THE RISE OF FEMALE LEADERSHIP
AND THE FUTURE OF BUSINESS

FORCE

OF

WOMEN
CEOS

ADRIANA LUNA CARLOS & HANNA OLIVAS
ALONG WITH 6 INSPIRING WOMEN CEOS

ISBN: 978-1-964619-13-2

Table of Contents

INTRODUCTION

"The Force of Women CEOs: The Rise of Female Leadership and The Future of Business" delves into these critical issues, seeking to uncover the reasons behind the glaring gender gap in corporate leadership. Beyond merely highlighting the problem, this book sets out to explore actionable strategies to usher in a new era of gender equality in the C-suite.

Research unequivocally demonstrates that companies helmed by women exhibit remarkable attributes. They not only achieve faster growth but also generate higher revenue, thereby fostering greater economic vitality and creating more job opportunities. This book examines how empowering more women to assume CEO roles can catalyze broader benefits for our economic system and society as a whole.

Moreover, the influence of women CEOs extends far beyond financial metrics. Their leadership style, characterized by collaboration over competition, injects fresh perspectives into organizational dynamics. By diversifying work cultures, women CEOs cultivate environments where innovation thrives and where inclusive decision-making leads to more successful and sustainable solutions.

As we embark on this exploration, "The Force of Women CEOs" invites you to journey through the stories of trailblazing women leaders who are reshaping industries and challenging norms. Together, let us uncover the transformative power of gender diversity at the highest levels of corporate leadership.

Hanna Olivas

Founder and CEO of She Rises Studios

https://www.linkedin.com/company/she-rises-studios/
https://www.facebook.com/sherisesstudios
https://www.instagram.com/sherisesstudios_llc/
www.SheRisesStudios.com

Author, Speaker, and Founder. Hanna was born and raised in Las Vegas, Nevada, and has paved her way to becoming one of the most influential women of 2022. Hanna is the co-founder of She Rises Studios and the founder of the Brave & Beautiful Blood Cancer Foundation. Her journey started in 2017 when she was first diagnosed with Multiple Myeloma, an incurable blood cancer. Now more than ever, her focus is to empower other women to become leaders because The Future is Female. She is currently traveling and speaking publicly to women to educate them on entrepreneurship, leadership, and owning the female power within.

THE FORCE OF A WOMAN CEO: MY JOURNEY AS CHIEF BRANDING OFFICER OF SHE RISES STUDIOS AND FENIX TV

By Hanna Olivas

In the bustling world of business, the image of a woman at the helm often evokes a powerful sense of resilience, determination, and innovation. As the Chief Branding Officer (CBO) of She Rises Studios and FENIX TV, I have navigated an extraordinary journey marked by profound challenges and remarkable victories.

This chapter is a reflection of that journey—a testament to the incredible importance of being a powerful woman in business, the struggles faced, the wins celebrated, and the invaluable lessons learned along the way.

The Beginning

Inception of She Rises Studios and FENIX TV Four years ago, the concept of She Rises Studios was born out of a profound need to create a platform that empowers women entrepreneurs. It wasn't just about building a business; it was about cultivating a community where women could find support, inspiration, and the tools necessary to thrive in a predominantly male-dominated arena.

FENIX TV, our dynamic extension into the world of media, emerged shortly after, driven by the same vision of amplifying women's voices and stories. Starting these ventures was anything but easy. As a woman CEO and CBO, I was often met with skepticism and doubt. The road to establishing credibility and respect was paved with countless sleepless nights, rigorous planning, and unwavering persistence.

I quickly learned that to succeed, I needed more than just a robust business plan—I needed a relentless belief in my vision and an unyielding commitment to bring it to life.

The Struggles

Battling Stereotypes and Building Credibility One of the most significant struggles I faced was breaking through the deeply entrenched stereotypes about women in leadership. The business world, despite its progress, still harbors biases that can be discouraging. Women CEOs are often perceived as less capable or less committed, assumptions that I had to continuously defy.

Building credibility required more than delivering results; it required proving, time and again, that my decisions and strategies were sound. Every setback was scrutinized more harshly, every success celebrated less enthusiastically. This constant pressure to perform can be exhausting, but it also becomes a powerful motivator. I learned to transform criticism into fuel, using it to drive myself and my team toward excellence.

The Wins

Celebrating Milestones and Impact Amidst the challenges, there were numerous victories that reaffirmed our mission and strengthened our resolve. Every successful project, every new partnership, and every story of transformation within our community was a win worth celebrating. These milestones were not just business achievements; they were indicators of the impact we were making in the lives of women entrepreneurs worldwide.

One particularly memorable win was the launch of our book, 'Women Who Lead - The Future of Entrepreneurship.' This project was a labor of love, showcasing the incredible journeys of women leaders who, like myself, had navigated the complexities of the business world. The overwhelming positive response we received was a testament to the power of storytelling and the importance of representation.

The Learnings

Adapting and Growing Every experience, whether a struggle or a win, brought with it invaluable lessons. One of the most critical learnings was the importance of adaptability. The business landscape is ever-evolving, and being rigid in approach can be detrimental. Embracing change and being willing to pivot when necessary became essential strategies for growth. Another key lesson was the significance of building a supportive network.

The journey of a woman CEO can often feel isolating, but surrounding oneself with like-minded individuals who understand and support your vision can make a world of difference. At She Rises Studios, we cultivated a community that not only empowered our members but also provided a robust support system for each other. The Role of a CEO: Leadership, Vision, and Resilience Being a CEO or CBO is not merely about holding a title; it is about embodying leadership, vision, and resilience. It requires the ability to inspire and motivate a team, to see beyond the immediate challenges, and to strategize for the future. It involves making difficult decisions, often under immense pressure, and standing by those decisions with confidence and conviction.

Leadership, especially as a woman, also entails empathy and understanding. It means recognizing the unique challenges faced by women in business and creating an environment where those challenges can be addressed and overcome. It is about being a role model, demonstrating through actions that success is attainable despite the obstacles.

Personal Reflections

The Journey of Self-Discovery My journey as the CBO of She Rises Studios and FENIX TV has been as much about personal growth as it has been about business success. It has been a path of self-discovery, where I have learned more about my strengths, my vulnerabilities, and my capabilities. It has taught me the importance of self-belief and the power of persistence. There were moments of doubt and fear, moments when the weight of responsibility felt overwhelming.

But each time, I found strength in the purpose that drove me. The vision of empowering women, of creating a legacy that would inspire future generations, kept me moving forward. The Importance of Empowerment and Representation At the heart of She Rises Studios and FENIX TV is the belief in the transformative power of empowerment and representation. When women see themselves reflected in positions of power and influence, it breaks down barriers and opens doors of possibility. It challenges societal norms and paves the way for a more inclusive and equitable business environment.

Our mission has always been to amplify the voices of women, to showcase their stories, and to provide them with the resources and support they need to succeed. This mission is not just about business; it is about creating a movement that redefines the narrative around women in leadership.

Strategies for Success: What It Takes to Lead a successful business requires a combination of strategic planning, innovative thinking, and unwavering determination. Here are some of the key strategies that have been instrumental in my journey

Vision and Purpose: Having a clear vision and a strong sense of purpose is crucial. It guides your decisions and keeps you focused on your goals.

Adaptability: The ability to adapt to changing circumstances and pivot when necessary is essential. The business world is dynamic, and flexibility can often be the difference between success and failure.

Building a Strong Team: Surround yourself with individuals who share your vision and are committed to the mission. A strong, cohesive team can achieve incredible things.

Resilience: Develop a resilient mindset. There will be setbacks and challenges, but resilience allows you to bounce back stronger and more determined.

Networking and Collaboration: Build a robust network of support. Collaborate with like-minded individuals and organizations to amplify your impact.

Continuous Learning: Never stop learning and growing. Seek out new knowledge, stay updated on industry trends, and be open to feedback and improvement.

Empathy and Understanding: Lead with empathy. Understand the unique challenges faced by your team and community, and work towards creating a supportive and inclusive environment.

Looking Ahead: The Future of Women in Business As I reflect on the past four years, I am filled with immense pride and gratitude for the journey we have undertaken. The growth of She Rises Studios and FENIX TV is a testament to the power of vision, resilience, and community. But our work is far from done.

The future holds endless possibilities for women in business. As we continue to break barriers and shatter glass ceilings, it is crucial to remain committed to the mission of empowerment and representation. We must continue to support each other, to lift each other up, and to create opportunities for future generations of women leaders.

In conclusion, being a powerful woman in business is not just about achieving success; it is about making a difference. It is about using your platform to inspire and empower others, to challenge the status quo, and to pave the way for a more inclusive and equitable world.

My journey as the CBO of She Rises Studios and FENIX TV has been a testament to this belief, and I am excited to see what the future holds for women entrepreneurs everywhere. As we move forward, let us remember that the force of a woman CEO is not just in her ability to lead, but in her ability to inspire, to empower, and to create a legacy of impact and change.

This is the true essence of leadership, and it is a journey that I am honored to be a part of.

My Personal Message To every woman reading this, remember that your journey is unique and valuable. Embrace your strengths, learn from your challenges, and never underestimate the power of your vision. The world needs your leadership, your innovation, and your resilience.

Together, we can create a future where women in business are not the exception but the norm. Let us rise together, let us lead together, and let us create a world where every woman has the opportunity to achieve her dreams and make a lasting impact. This is our time, and we are unstoppable. This chapter is a reflection of my journey, but it is also a call to action for all women who aspire to lead.

Believe in yourself, embrace your power, and never stop striving for greatness. The force of a woman CEO is a force that can change the world, and together, we will make it happen!

Adriana Luna Carlos

Founder and CEO of She Rises Studios & FENIX TV

https://www.linkedin.com/in/adriana-luna-carlos/
https://www.facebook.com/adrianalunacarlos
https://www.instagram.com/sherisesstudios_llc/
https://www.sherisesstudios.com/
https://www.srslatina.com/
https://fenixtv.app/

Adriana Luna Carlos is an accomplished web and graphic designer, author, and mentor with a passion for helping women succeed in life and business. With over 10 years of experience in graphic and web arts, Adriana has built a reputation as an innovative leader and entrepreneur. In 2020, she co-founded She Rises Studios, a multi-digital media company and publishing house that has helped countless clients achieve their branding and marketing goals. In 2023, she co-created FENIX TV, an online streaming platform that showcases stories of people breaking barriers, shattering stereotypes, and triumphing against the odds.

As an advocate for women's success, Adriana challenges her clients and mentees to strive for nothing less than excellence. She has a deep understanding of the insecurities and challenges that women often face in the business world and provides the guidance and resources needed to overcome them. Her success as a business leader and entrepreneur has made her a sought-after mentor and speaker at events around the world.

Through her work, Adriana has demonstrated a commitment to creating opportunities for women to succeed in business and life. Her passion for innovation, leadership, and women's empowerment has made her a respected figure in the business community, and her impact will undoubtedly continue to inspire and empower women for years to come.

LEADERSHIP IN ACTION:
INSPIRING THROUGH EXAMPLE

By Adriana Luna Carlos

Being a CEO isn't just about running a company—it's about embodying leadership in every decision and action. It requires vision, resilience, and the ability to inspire others toward a common goal. As leaders at She Rises Studios, we've learned that true leadership means leading by example, fostering a culture of trust and collaboration, and always striving to learn and improve. It's about making tough decisions with integrity, empowering your team to innovate, and staying grounded in your mission. Being a CEO means embracing challenges as opportunities for growth, and most importantly, believing in the potential of your team and the impact of your work.

My journey into entrepreneurship began with deep-rooted lessons from my family. Raised in an environment where entrepreneurship was more than a career—it was a way of life—I absorbed invaluable insights into financial management and resilience. These early teachings weren't just about theory; they were practical skills that became my compass as I embarked on building my own business. From the start, I faced the challenge of balancing big dreams with the realities of starting a business. Dreaming big is crucial, but it's the hard work and smart decisions that turn those dreams into something real. Entrepreneurship isn't just about running a business; it's a journey that reshapes your whole perspective on life. It's about facing challenges head-on and growing stronger with each obstacle.

One of the toughest lessons I learned early on was resilience. In the business world, setbacks are inevitable—whether it's financial struggles or market uncertainties. Each setback became a chance for me to learn, adapt, and come back stronger. It's not just about bouncing back from failures; it's about using those experiences to grow personally and professionally. Through these challenges, I discovered my true strengths and weaknesses, gaining a deeper understanding of what drives me forward. This journey of self-discovery has given me the confidence to make bold decisions, not just in business but in every aspect of life. Being an entrepreneur isn't just about making money; it's about creating something meaningful and inspiring others to do the same.

Every day brings new lessons in entrepreneurship. It's not just about managing finances or marketing strategies; it's about constantly learning and adapting to new situations. Creativity is at the heart of entrepreneurship—it's about thinking outside the box and finding innovative solutions to problems. Whether it's developing a new product or finding a better way to connect with customers, this creativity keeps the journey exciting and fulfilling. As a woman CEO, I'm not just building a business; I'm building a legacy. Whether it's passing on a family business to the next generation or creating a company that makes a lasting impact, entrepreneurship gives me a sense of purpose and drive.

Financial empowerment has been crucial on my journey. Learning how to manage finances wisely and invest strategically has been key to building a strong foundation for my business. It's not just about making money; it's about feeling confident in my financial decisions and planning for the future. Overcoming setbacks has taught me the importance of a growth mindset—seeing challenges as opportunities for learning and growth. Surrounding myself with mentors and a supportive community has been essential in staying resilient and motivated during tough times. Taking care of my well-being—both physically and mentally—has also been crucial in sustaining my energy and focus.

Looking back on our journey with She Rises Studios, it's clear that our path wasn't just about starting a business—it was about finding a way to support women when they needed it most. We launched our studio right in the middle of a global pandemic, not just to help others, but because we were searching for a community ourselves. Our goal has always been to inspire, empower, and educate women facing tough times, guiding them with hope, strength, and the belief that together, we are stronger.

Navigating Challenges and Embracing Growth

Starting She Rises Studios was far from easy. With no initial money and full-time jobs on top of it all, the first year was a blur of hard work and sleepless nights. We had to get creative to raise the money we needed and build our business from scratch. Looking back, I wish I had known sooner how important it is to see challenges as chances to grow. Every late night and sacrifice we made taught us that pushing through tough times is key to turning setbacks into successes.

The Role of Grit and Resilience in Success

Our journey from a small startup to a global team impacting women in 22 countries has been all about grit and resilience. Supporting thousands of women each year and seeing their progress has been incredibly rewarding. Leading a team of 23 people scattered across the globe has taught us the power of perseverance and teamwork. It's not just about bouncing back when things go wrong—it's about sticking to your vision no matter what. Our journey shows that with determination, you can achieve incredible things.

Learning from Mistakes and Celebrating Milestones

One of our biggest lessons came from a funny mistake early on when I forgot to hit record during an interview with Laura Trump. It was a tech blunder that taught me the importance of attention to detail and humility in admitting mistakes. Every milestone we reached, from launching impactful campaigns to expanding internationally, taught us the value of learning from failures. I wish I had known earlier that mistakes are opportunities to learn and grow. Embracing setbacks and using them to improve is crucial to succeeding as a founder.

Building a Community and Making a Difference

At She Rises Studios, our success is built on creating a supportive community for women. We believe in collaboration over competition, creating a space where women can share their stories and support each other. Seeing women heal from trauma and overcome challenges through our platform has been incredibly fulfilling. Building a strong community around your vision is essential as a founder—having people who believe in your mission can help you through tough times and ensure long-term success.

Balancing Vision with Adaptability

One of the hardest parts of starting a business is balancing your vision with being open to change. I wish I had understood sooner how important it is to stay flexible and willing to adjust your plans. Over the years, we've learned to listen to feedback, adapt our strategies, and grow with our community's needs. Founders should hold onto their vision while being ready to pivot when necessary. Flexibility and adaptability are crucial for navigating the ups and downs of entrepreneurship and achieving lasting success.

My CEO journey has taught me that resilience, community, and staying true to our mission are keys to success. From our humble beginnings during a global crisis to becoming a global force for women's empowerment, every challenge has been a chance to grow. As we look ahead, we're committed to expanding our impact and empowering women worldwide. We believe in the endless potential of women to create positive change, showing that when women rise together, we all rise.

Jacqueline L. Long, MA, MPA, MS

Elevate Your Biz Digital Consulting, LLC
CEO/Business Marketing Strategist

https://www.elevatedfemales.com
https://instagram.com/elevateyourbizllc
https://www.elevateyourbizcoaching.com

Jacqueline is a Business Marketing Strategist, Podcast Host, Master Certified Life, Transformation & Mindset Coach, to female entrepreneurs. She is also the Co-author of two Anthologies for women in business, Purpose Driven Paycheck and Becoming an Unstoppable Woman Entrepreneur II. Over the last several years, Jacqueline has helped women start and scale their coaching businesses, breakthrough their limiting beliefs and master their sales and marketing strategies online. She is currently in the process of transitioning her business to specialize in book writing/coaching, digital course creation and podcast marketing for women in business. Jacqueline is the founder of Elevate Your Biz Digital Consulting, LLC - her official brand dedicated to women achieving the next level of their dreams, by building profitable online businesses. Jacqueline holds three advanced degrees (Master of Science in Human Resources Management, Master of Public Administration & Master of Arts in Criminal Justice). Prior to starting her coaching business 7 years ago, she had a 20+ year career in non-profit senior management. She has formerly served as a Director of Case Management, Director of Social Services, Director of Clinical Trials, and Vice President of Human resources. Jacqueline is a native New Yorker who enjoys traveling, reading, journaling, and spending time with her large family. She has two young adult daughters, who are graduate students, and she lives in the Atlanta Metro-Area.

LESSONS IN LEADERSHIP: WORDS OF WISDOM FOR NEW & ASPIRING FEMALE LEADERS & CEOS

By Jacqueline L. Long, MA, MPA, MS

"Leadership is about making others better as a result of your presence, and making sure that impact lasts in your absence."
– Sheryl Sandberg, former COO Facebook

To all the women leaders throughout time, who have trail-blazed, broken glass ceilings, and opened new doors for us as women, thank you! For all the women who today are leading and demonstrating the force of women CEOs, while fostering change and making a difference, you're killing it! And finally, to all the new and aspiring female leaders of tomorrow—you can do this!

We need more strong, talented, transformational women in leadership/ entrepreneurial positions, breaking new glass ceilings and forging future paths for women CEOs and leaders. Therefore, this chapter is dedicated to the NEW first-time or aspiring female leader/CEO, who's elevating and becoming the fierce, fabulous force in leadership that she was meant to be. I share my own experiences, offer recommendations on the leadership skills needed to be successful, along with words of wisdom to encourage you to become an exceptional female leader or CEO. I hope this chapter inspires you in some small or significant way.

What is Leadership?

I strongly believe that becoming a dynamic and transformative leader starts with educating ourselves about what leadership is and how we can improve in order to better support those we lead. Therefore, let's start with the question, what is *leadership*? According to the Oxford online dictionary, *leadership* is "the action of leading a group of people or an organization." For this chapter, I will use the terms *CEO, manager/executive, and leader* interchangeably. However, the term *leadership* will be used to discuss and describe the skill or art of leading or influencing others to accomplish a collective goal.

One of the major causes of failed businesses, failed organizational goals, and poor staff performance is poor leadership. According to Northhouse (2025), a major challenge for many in leadership is that they do not understand the meaning or nature of leadership. Leadership is important to organizational and employee success. Stronger leaders mean better staff, business, and organizational performance. Therefore, it's important to learn what leadership is and the scholarly theories that help to explain leadership styles and how to incorporate them into developing leadership skills and leading transformational organizations.

Several major scholarly leadership schools of thought that also help us to understand the characteristics and styles that are essential to leading. Some major leadership theoretical schools of thought include: trait theories, which argue that some people are born with inherent characteristics and traits that make them natural leaders; contingency/situational leadership theories, which focus on the leader implementing a course of action based on the situation and/or environment; behavioral theories, which assert that leaders are not born, they are made through learning and are developed over time; and finally there are participative/managerial and relationships theories, such as transformational leadership, which assert that the best leadership styles focus on developing relationships between leaders and followers, effective supervision, participation, investment, and contribution of group members in the leadership decision-making process (Northhouse, 2025). Many experienced leaders ground and adapt their leadership styles in one or a combination of these leadership theories. For example, I think of myself as a participative, situational, and transformational leader. I focus on the importance of people contributing to the process, the situation that I'm leading and what it requires, as well as the importance of teamwork and relationships in getting a job done. While I do believe that some people are born with inherent leadership characteristics, as some theories have held, I also believe that great leadership can be learned. Transformational leadership is about a leader's successful and skilled ability to influence, inspire, coach, and support others in achieving a common goal, in a cooperative and participatory way. To do this effectively takes a leader with patience, clarity, trust, skill, and an understanding of human behavior. It takes flexibility and effective communication. Good leaders understand this and strive to achieve it.

Women in Leadership

Historically, women were not thought of as having the ability, skills, temperament, or knowledge to become executives and CEOs. However, women have progressed over time and made strides into entering traditionally male-dominated professional fields, including leadership and executive positions. Chamorro-Pemuzic (2021) argues that although women consistently outperform men in the traits of effective leaders, over time, women are still underrepresented in leadership and executive roles. Unfortunately, in male-dominated corporations, women are often thought to not be "as good as men" in terms of leadership abilities.

Over the last several decades, however, women have proven that many of the old leadership stereotypes are wrong. Women are breaking through the glass ceiling and becoming leadership executives and CEOs at a rising rate. In fact, Hinchcliffe (2023) holds that, "...[F]or the first time in the Fortune 500 list's 68-year history, more than 10 percent of Fortune 500 companies are now led by women." Women today are holding our own and moving into C-suite positions, leading organizations as CEOs and becoming the CEOs of their own businesses. However, while there has been progress, a lack of equality in leadership roles and barriers to entry still exist for some women (Rhode, 2017). More specifically, Craven (2023) holds that 4.4% of Black women work in management. But only 1.4% are executives, or members of the C-suite. And many executive boards do not reflect the diversity of their workforce. Therefore, while women have made progress in executive and leadership roles, there is still room for additional progress and growth. There is an ongoing need for more women and women of color in leadership and C-suite positions to reflect diversity, and improve and strengthen organizational productivity and goals.

My Story

So how did I start my journey as a professional and female leader? Here's my story and journey. I'm the youngest of fourteen children. My parents were of mixed African, Asian and European ancestry, from the Caribbean twin islands of Trinidad and Tobago. I was raised by my mom, with the help of my stepfather, in the tough neighborhood of Brooklyn, NY. My mother worked as a nurse's aid and in the early to mid 80's, owned an Indo-Caribbean Roti restaurant in Brooklyn. However, in this community, the expectation for young minority girls and boys was not positive. Many fell hard to drugs, teenage pregnancy, trouble with the law, or death. Growing up, there was no expectation or push for me to go to college. I was just expected to work hard at whatever I did. My mother was strict and I was surrounded by many role models in my early years, including my mom, stepdad, aunts, and uncles who had left the homeland for a better life, or "The American dream."

My first year of high school was a mess. I disliked my school and had a hard time adjusting. I struggled with my classes and felt isolated. By the Spring term of my freshman year, I had lost interest in school, fallen behind in my classes and considered dropping out. When mom discovered it, she intervened early. Mom changed my school and sent me to a small alternative high school, where I could make up credits and get back on track. She tightened her supervision of me and made every effort to keep me out of the neighborhood and expose me to experiences and things outside of the community that would support my success. This may sound cliché, but I truly believe that this made a significant difference in who I'd eventually become.

In my sophomore year of high school, I straightened up. I studied hard, joined the leadership club and other extracurricular activities, and then was voted student body president in my junior year. I would end up achieving straight A's through my senior year and graduating Valedictorian of my high school class. I hadn't thought about these early experiences in a while. But reflecting on them, I can clearly see now that a career in leadership was early in the making for me.

An Unexpected Career Path

I didn't start my career wanting to be a leader or CEO of a company. I had no idea really what I wanted to do growing up. I originally thought I wanted to be a singer (a story for another day and time). But that wasn't practical. I enjoyed music, but it wasn't really my passion. I had no idea what I enjoyed, or what I was good at doing. So, I did what everyone else did when you don't really know what to do with your life…I went to college. I would go on to become the first in my family to do many things. As a first-generation American, I would become the first to graduate with both college and graduate degrees. I would also be the first to pursue a PhD and become the CEO of my own online business.

Before starting my business, I had a 20-year career in the nonprofit sector, as a mental health case worker and HIV/AIDS pre/post-test counselor, working with the Criminal Justice population. I moved up after two years to the position of HIV Case Management Supervisor while working on my first graduate degree. I worked hard and moved up again to several different senior-level leadership and management positions during my career: Director of Social Services, Director of Case Management, and Vice President of Human Resources.

In 2013, I found myself burnt out, bored, and wanting a change and new direction in my career. After all that I had accomplished, the over-achiever in me wanted more. And so, I made a life-changing decision. I left a well-paying position, moved my family to Georgia, and started a new life. Then, in the Spring of 2015, I would put my leadership skills to the ultimate test. I would start my own online coaching and consulting business. And here I am today, the CEO of my own business, with a wealth of knowledge and a lot of hard knocks from learning in the "trenches." And I have no regrets.

Challenges, Mistakes, and Lessons Learned

As I mentioned previously, I really didn't think of leadership and management as a career. And when I started, I was clueless. I really had no idea what I was doing or how to be a good leader or manager. The reality is that no academic program can truly prepare you for the complexities of leading and being an effective leader. Studying leadership can provide you with the foundation to build from. But becoming an effective, transformative leader is developed with a combination of education, skill, experience and on the job learning.

I experienced many challenges in my positions over the years, including long-term staff resistance to new management and ideas, management politics, managing cultural diversity, managing with no senior-level support, managing with little resources, terminating staff for the first time, burnout, micro-aggressions from male colleagues, being the only woman senior manager in the C-suite, as well as being the only Black woman in senior management. The most challenging issues were dealing with consistent staff turnover and budget cuts, where we had to do more with fewer available resources. This was a very common occurrence in the nonprofit sector. But managing sexism in the workplace was the worst.

I specifically remember one experience when I was a Director of Case Management. A male co-worker, the CFO of the organization, walked into my office to discuss the program budget. He opened my closed office door and walked right into my office without knocking. When I asked why he hadn't knocked before entering, he responded, "You're not at home. Why is your office door closed?" When asked if he would do the same to the CEO, he didn't reply. I was very aware that my colleague was of a cultural background and religion that did not view women as equals in general, especially not as managers or leaders. So, I had to manage this, while stepping into my own as a manager and leader.

Another issue I had to manage was, the CEO and CFO occasionally having management and organizational meetings amongst themselves, excluding me, the only female member of the management team. I would sometimes receive an email later, telling me what I was required to do. This was an issue I had to address directly, with them. I was then viewed as being "overly sensitive" about it. However, I had a goal and timeline for what I wanted to learn and gain from the organization. Therefore, I didn't throw in the towel. I used it as best I could, to my advantage and learned how to deal with the micro-aggressions and sexism. I stayed, I learned, I got better at my job, and demanded respect and to be treated on equal terms. I stayed with that organization for four years and then moved on to a better opportunity.

I had other experiences, at different organizations, where I dealt with management politics, discrimination and was overlooked for senior management positions that I was overqualified for. I put in many years of hard work, with many hours of overtime working in organizations that didn't always appreciate my talent. I often had to advocate for myself and prove my managerial and leadership "worthiness", as a woman and specifically as a Black woman. There were many times that I was passed over. Once, I was even asked to train my new boss. A request I respectfully refused. It was questionable how I could be qualified to train a superior on what to do, but I wasn't qualified enough for the position, no matter my extensive qualifications and experience. I had to face the reality that in some organizations, CEO and higher-level leadership positions were not reachable for me. If I wanted more, I would have to wait it out, take my skills and experience elsewhere, or create the opportunity myself. And so, that was part of the inspiration that led to the start Elevate Your Biz Coaching and Consulting.

Being a leader or C-Suite executive, you're inclined to make mistakes along the way. I didn't make any disastrous errors. But I did get things wrong sometimes. My mistakes included things like not delegating enough, hiring the wrong staff, losing my temper, making the wrong decision, and not being clear in my expectations. In the early years, I either micro-managed or didn't manage enough, until I learned how to trust my team, delegate more, and find my management style as a leader.

The important lessons that I learned during the process, however, are that setbacks, failures, and mistakes are part of the process. Instead of giving up or beating myself up, I identified my weaknesses and learning gaps, got crystal clear about what I wanted, improved my skills, toughened my skin, and kept going. I also learned to identify when a position or organization was a dead end, and had no opportunity for growth or advancement. This happens. So keep this in mind and don't get complacent. Learn when it's time to move on, grow and take your talents elsewhere. And when there's limited opportunity, don't be afraid to create one. You're a leader and that's what we do. We lead and create opportunities.

Words of Wisdom for Success

What does it take to become a successful, formidable female leader and CEO?

Simply- it's the desire to be one and the commitment and fortitude to do it well. Leadership is not only about influencing others, but it is also about taking responsibility for leading ourselves and creating our own professional paths. Below I share some important skills from my experience as a leader and manager, for new managers and female CEOs/entrepreneurs that I believe will support your success:

- *Hone/polish your decision-making skills* – Decision-making is 90% of your job as a leader. You'll often have to make hard decisions under pressure. Don't waiver, don't procrastinate, and don't overthink things. Build your confidence and learn how to assess a situation, gather as much information as you need, weigh the pros and cons, and make decisions quickly. This skill will get better every time you use it. Sound decision-making makes great leaders.

- *Learn how to problem solve* – As a leader, you'll be faced with problems almost daily. This will be at least half of what you do from day to day. Assess the problem and aim to solve it for the best possible outcome, and not for perfection.

- *Assess your skills & Learning Gaps* – Your job is to know what you do well and to know what you don't know. Keep your expertise, knowledge, skills, and areas of needed improvement up to date.

- *Master communication* – Learn how to communicate clearly and concisely, both written and verbal. Your communication skills are an essential part of your role as a leader. Master them.

- *Embrace fear* – Leadership is scary and uncomfortable. But it's also rewarding and fulfilling. Be scared. But take action anyway. You'll either get it right or learn how to do it better the next time. Fear is your internal signal that you're stepping out of your comfort zone and growing. Don't resist it. Roll with it.

- *Fail forward* – The possibility of failure is inherent to anything we do. Accept that failure can and may happen. However, don't get stuck. Your job is to use your failure as a learning experience and keep moving forward.

- *Get a mentor* – Leadership can be lonely. Having a mentor can be an invaluable source of support. You can learn from this person, bounce ideas off them, set and share your goals with them, and get advice when needed. This can be extremely helpful to your growth.

- *Be resourceful*- Leaders lead others and themselves. They don't wait for others to obtain what they need. Be resourceful and find answers to questions or information you need.

- *Commit to ongoing learning* – Your team and business are only as good as you are. Technology and business are changing every day. It's your job to keep up. The more you know, the more knowledge and capital you invest in yourself and your business. As a leader, your job is to stay current on what's happening in your industry and to teach and train your team. Work on developing and continuing your job knowledge and your managerial and leadership skills. Keep growing and learning things.

- *Set boundaries* – Establish clear boundaries in business. Always be clear about expectations and roles and hold others accountable.

- *Be open to feedback and constructive criticism* – Feedback and criticism can be difficult for many, especially leaders. But it's essential to your success. To get better you must know what you're doing well and where you need to grow and improve. Therefore, be open to feedback/constructive criticism. Don't take anything personally. Think of it as part of your continued development. You need it to get to the next level.

- *Delegate, delegate, delegate* – Delegation is essential to leadership success. You can't and shouldn't be doing it all. Learn to delegate effectively. Trust in the competency of your staff. Delegate, be clear, set deadlines, establish roles and responsibility for tasks, determine outcomes and expectations, set up channels of communication and check-in dates. Hold yourself and your team accountable. Then, let go and be supportive and available if/when needed. Your staff will love you for it.

- *Embrace diversity and inclusion* – Support diversity in your organization. Develop a diversity statement that clearly describes your mission and commitment to diversity. Train and support staff in inclusiveness.

- *Surround yourself with like-minded women* – Create a support system and network of women leaders/CEOs that you can turn to for support and learn from.

- *Sharpen your self-awareness* – Self-awareness is the first step to growth. Get to know yourself, your likes/dislikes, weaknesses/strengths, triggers, skill sets, etc. Having self-awareness will make you a more confident and intentional leader. To know yourself is to better understand others.

- *Master your mindset* – Mindset is about the way you think. It's about the thoughts - mostly the negative and limiting thoughts that enter your mind and often hold you back/limit you from taking action or making decisions. The cliché saying goes, whatever you think, you're right. Think, I can do anything…and you will.

- *Finally, be confident, adaptable, flexible, patient, kind, caring, and inspiring. These are simply some of the basic and best qualities a leader can have.*

Conclusion

I've shared a lot of skills here that will be useful and important to your development as a female leader. However, this list isn't exhaustive by any means. There are many more that you will learn and acquire as you gain more experience along the way. Remember leadership is both a privilege and a responsibility. Take it seriously, and work on your growth consistently.

I have been honest in sharing my experience and story because I was once a new manager/leader. And after twenty-five years of experience, I'm not perfect by any means. No leader is. I'm still learning every day because I have a passion for what I do, and I'm committed to business leadership. I'm not a know-it-all leader/businesswoman who has earned a ton of degrees and thinks no one can tell me or teach me how to become a better CEO or executive. I'm quite the opposite. I'm a lifelong learner who believes in introspection, ongoing growth, constructive feedback, and learning from my mentors to do better and be better. I want you to understand that while I made mistakes and was faced with many challenges, it's par for the course and I learned a ton. I mostly learned about myself and how to be a better woman, so that I could become a better leader and person. I learned how to fail forward and pick myself up, to embrace fear, to challenge myself, and to never give up. I've learned my strengths and I've learned my weaknesses. But most importantly, I learned the gift of passion and humility.

I've discussed leadership and the state of women in leadership today to show that women are demonstrating that we are not only competent executives and leaders, but we can also be as good as, and even better leaders than men. I also shared my own journey to show that it can be challenging. But if it weren't tough, it wouldn't be worth the work. I've come a long way, but I'm still evolving and elevating. I now look forward to the opportunity to support new and upcoming women CEOs/entrepreneurs in my business and in my future college teaching.

My final parting words of wisdom for new women CEOs and leaders are, be confident, always believe in yourself and your abilities, be bold, be assertive, invest in yourself, hold yourself accountable, and never stop learning and growing. But most importantly, lead with passion and heart. Enjoy the journey.

Elevate!

REFERENCES

1. Chamorro-Pemuzic, T. (2021, March 7). If Women are Better Leaders, Then Why are they Not in Charge? Forbes.com https://www.forbes.com/sites/tomaspremuzic/2021/03/07/if-women-are-better-leaders-then-why-are-they-not-in-charge/?sh=60df45256c88

2. **Craven-Richard, M. (2023, October 19). We Need More Black Women in the C-Suite. Here's Why. Forbes.com. https://www.forbes.com/sites/mayarichard-craven/2023/10/19/we-need-more-black-women-in-the-c-suite-heres-why/?sh=3887c97561f4**

3. Hinchcliffe, E (2023, January 20). Women Run More than 10% of Fortune 500 Companies for the First Time. Shrm.com. https://www.shrm.org/executive-network/insights/women-run-10-fortune-500-companies-first-time

4. Northhouse, P. G. (2015). Leadership: Theory and Practice, 7th Edition. SAGE Publications, Inc.

5. Oxford Dictionary (2024). Leadership. (N.d).

6. Rhode, D. L. (2017). *Women and leadership*. Oxford University Press.

Dr. Real N. Kunene, MBA

CEO of Rise to Greater Heights Network

https://www.linkedin.com/in/dr-real-n-kunene-mba-5b809418
https://www.facebook.com/RisetoGreaterHeights/
https://www.instagram.com/rise_to_greater_heights/
https://swaticanadianinternational.ca/
https://risetogreaterheights.com/

Dr. Real N. Kunene, MBA. Governance, Diplomacy and Protocol Specialist * Certified Les Brown Motivational Speaker. Dr. Nompumelelo Real Kunene is an International Human Rights Policy Analyst and a Governance, Diplomacy and Protocol Specialist. This passionate leader holds a Ph.D. with a discipline in Leadership and Business. From owning two diverse companies to having experience as a CEO, and guiding Fortune 100 companies to helping multi-million-dollar enterprises, Dr. Kunene has a distinctive talent for empowering high-achieving coaches, elite startups, and leaders to become dominant forces in their industries. Dr. Kunene is an Award-Winning Author, 10x Number 1 Amazon and International bestselling author. But she doesn't stop there! Real is the voice behind the award-winning international podcast: Rise to Greater Heights Network, and she's also a highly sought after energetic certified Les Brown International speaker. Connect with her, and get ready to RISE TO GREATER HEIGHTS.

RISE TO GREATER HEIGHTS

By Dr. Real N. Kunene, MBA

"The sky is no longer your limit, but your point of view...SO, let's all RISE TO GREATER HEIGHTS."
—Dr. Real N. Kunene

Many leaders are failing to promote a sense of trust in their employees, but to be able to cultivate crucial traits is what makes a leader! Delegation and empowerment are central to effective leadership and most clearly demonstrate who has "the leader gene." I had always enjoyed leading people, be it in projects or coaching calls, but, like anyone else, it took practice for me to develop my leadership skills. Regardless of whether you've worked your way up the corporate ladder or just started your own business, leaders must have specific abilities and foster the development of certain qualities. To help you accomplish improved outcomes for your company and make you a better leader, please keep reading.

Delegation and Empowerment

Delegating is one of the fundamental obligations of a leader; you need to concentrate on key responsibilities while leaving the rest to others. Your ability to get everyone working and pulling together is vital to your success. A good leader has confidence in their capacity to prepare and grow the employees under them. Irrespective of the condition and stance you are in, no single individual can achieve everything at once, and leaders understand this before anyone else does. They have the eagerness to encourage those they lead to act independently. Always remember that you can't do everything on your own. Therefore, great leaders manage to delegate smaller tasks to their team members while directing their focus toward major tasks. Good leaders recognize that delegation does more than merely assign the job to someone else; it encourages their followers as well. The purpose isn't just to free yourself up and increase the collaboration of others but to lead to better decision-making that helps your direct reports develop.

Delegation is simply about sharing responsibilities. As a diplomacy and protocol specialist, I work with organizations to define meeting and event procedures. My work primarily emphasizes the creation of protocol standards that uphold traditions and ensure participants display politeness and respect. I plan and implement events and functions for senior personnel including foreign dignitaries, diplomats, and foreign military personnel. As a leader in this role, I have to make sure to establish and maintain liaison with officials of government ministries and other agencies, consular and diplomatic representatives, and private sector organizations and undertake research in protocol policy and procedures.

Leadership is the capability to get people to work for you because they *want* to, and delegating to others shows that you have faith in their skills. This can result in constructive confidence in the workplace. Your employees want to feel respected and trusted. With this, they are more likely to make decisions that are in the best interest of the company and the customer. When employees are encouraged, they usually feel grateful that they got chosen, and they feel the significance of being part of the company. On the other hand, leaders who continue to micromanage impede the skills of their team members, and it can create a lack of confidence, and, more importantly, often leads to poor outcomes. If you continue to micromanage your subordinates, you will not be able to concentrate on significant matters, so delegate errands to your subordinates and see how they accomplish their tasks. Trusting that your employees can manage the assignment given to them is vital to the effortless operation of the organization.

Leaders who nail delegation know they can't do everything alone, and more importantly, they don't have to. I am also a resilience to greatness coach who **empowers** motivated professionals and entrepreneurs with the tools they need to RISE TO GREATER HEIGHTS in their wealth, health, and relationships. I have helped everyone from motivated professionals, government officials, public figures, psychiatrists, executives, authors, and entrepreneurs to coaches to unlock their full potential. One of the most distinctive features about me is that I have been personally mentored, trained, and coached by the world's leading motivational speaker, Les Brown (with his high-impact, customized message and standing ovation), and I've been motivated and trained to be an achiever and leader with the mentality of Not Over Until You Win.

Here's what Les Brown says: "Hi, my name is Les Brown, international motivational speaker and trainer. I highly recommend Ms. Kunene's training for entrepreneurs, executives, and professionals. Ms. Kunene is a powerhouse of a young lady. I really respect her tenacity and determination to take charge of her destiny. It has been said that success leaves clues. Real has shared the many lessons she has learned along her road to success as an entrepreneur."

Delegation is the cornerstone of effective leadership, but what does it really mean? At its core, delegation is about sharing the workload and responsibilities. So, my ultimate goal for anyone who comes in contact with me is for them to feel extremely confident and excited about their offer. From early-stage startups and entrepreneurs to C-suite executives, I offer professional development tools to increase productivity, improve communication, and improve bottom-line results. I believe that great leaders not only inspire their employees but also provide them with all the resources to accomplish the goal and allow them to bear the responsibility. In this way, you exhibit a sense of trust, which helps inspire your team to work better and lets your team members know that they are totally up to any challenges they face.

Vision and Purpose

Effective delegation is a win-win for both leaders and their teams. Having a clear vision transforms the individual into a unique kind of person; they not only envision the future themselves but share their idea with their supporters. Great leaders have a dream; not only are they able to view a situation, but they are enthusiastic about their work. They are dedicated enough to accomplish their intended outcomes at any cost. Once prepared, audacity allows leaders to push things in the right direction so that high performance is easily achieved. Rather than preventing difficulties, they focus on all exceptional matters, create policies, and examine the efficacy of company strategies. When tested, they don't give in too quickly, but they have an exhilarating notion of where they are going and what they are attempting to achieve. Therefore, leaders should also be self-driven; such commitment is necessary since it inspires a sense of accountability in the team members to work harder at aiming to accomplish better outcomes for the company.

The fear of losing control and thus of failure can be a daunting obstacle to effective delegation. As an advocate for human rights, I encourage change makers and educate them on the issues at hand so that their voices can be heard, too. I work with the individuals in charge, listening closely before calling out issues that need change. I serve not just as a vocal protester, but I go one step further by encouraging these changes through education rather than merely telling government leaders why something needs fixing (which happens quite frequently). So, my organization fills a critical role in society by providing valuable services that governments may not always be able to deliver. From poverty relief to human rights advocacy, my organization is vital for supporting the most vulnerable members of my community.

In leadership, empowerment serves as the catalyst for transformation. A good leader is usually motivated, and employees are easily attracted to them and feel more positive as a result. Focused, exceptional leaders plan everything on time, and this value of vision changes a transactional manager into an influential leader because they consider the potential consequences of their decisions and determine approaches and practices that strengthen the idea. Not only are the best leaders positive, but their confidence is transmissible, as they plug into the passions of their employees. A great leader goes above and gives responsibilities to their best shot, because it will not only earn the admiration of their team members, but it will also inspire a new sense of power in them. In general, a leader's job is not limited to getting a job done; instead, they are the guiding influence on the team and someone the team can look up to because they are full of enthusiasm and dedication.

Honesty and Integrity

The ultimate value of leadership is undeniably honesty, whether it's giving appropriate recognition for achievements or placing security and excellence first. Great leaders always demonstrate integrity, and without honesty, the organization won't achieve feasible success, so remember to lead by example. Integrity is one of the traits that define a good leader. Leaders exemplify these principles so blatantly that no employee questions their reliability for a minute. Honesty and moral values mirrored by leadership in any organization are a manifestation of yourself. If you make explicit and ethical conduct a significant value, your team will follow.

A great leader is one who sticks with the truth and inspires their people by establishing high but achievable requirements and opportunities. Make sure your organization emphasizes the significance of honesty to leaders at different levels to see how reasonable one can be when everyone around them is deceitful. When you are accountable for a team of people, it is essential to be honest. Thus, fairness and truthfulness are the two primary components that make a good leader.

Leaders prosper when they stick to their principles by doing what's right, even if that isn't the best thing for the existing plan or even the bottom line. Honesty is vital for the individual and the organization. Leaders should be particularly ethical and consider that integrity and consistency form the basis of success. Though it may not certainly be a metric in employee appraisals, honest, influential leaders treat people the way they want to be treated. Honesty is a consistent behavior rather than something situational. It's critical for top-level directors who are making numerous other substantial decisions. Leaders should not be able to decide when to lie and when to tell the truth; great leaders represent the principles they want to see in their teams and urge everyone to follow suit. The true mark of leadership operates as a model for how every employee should behave while allowing leeway to follow those objectives and become the best employees they can conceivably be. As expressed, integrity and trustworthiness form the basis of success. These are the most critical leadership traits that empower leaders to stand up for what they believe in.

Motivation

Perhaps the most challenging job for a leader is to encourage others to follow, but for the economy, great leaders inspire others to do more. Put it all together, and what develops is a picture of the genuinely motivating leader who challenges their people by setting high but attainable principles. Inspiring is a value that describes a good leader; organizations must discover the best ways to cultivate these essential qualities in current and developing leaders. Being able to motivate your team is great for concentrating on the company's concept and targets, and as a leader, you should be optimistic. This positive attitude should be evident through your actions. The best leaders are a foundation of upbeat power; they always seem to have an answer and still know what to say to motivate and restore confidence. When the going gets tough, having the quality of audacity means that you are inclined to take risks in the pursuit of the success of your goals with no guarantee of achievement, and your team looks up to you and sees how you respond to the condition.

Individuals become leaders because they are enthusiastic about their careers and avoid personal condemnation but look for avenues to increase harmony and get people to work together effectively and successfully as a team. A constructive position and an honest concern for the well-being of their employees is yet another characteristic of great leaders because there is no assurance in life or business—every decision you make involves a risk of some kind. All these traits are essential to excellent management because these individuals love what they do, and always know what to say to motivate and encourage the same amount of enthusiasm in other people. While a passionate attitude can never act as a replacement for other leadership qualities, it is your job to keep spirits up, and that begins with an admiration for the hard work that they have put in. If you are competent in motivating your subordinates, you can easily surmount any existing or potential challenge because you have an innovative concept and know how to transform your ideas into real-world success stories.

Self-Awareness and Humility

While this is a more focused skill, leaders know that there are apparent differences between management and employees. Self-awareness is the utmost for leadership, so use this expertise to maintain a professional and objective distance for the best interests of the organization. Great leaders are those who are pivotal but also respectful, and that is why the leadership styles most great leaders embrace put lots of weight on team dynamics instead of focusing on self-promotion. A good leader is always noble and always thinks about their followers since pride won't get in the way of collecting information; they need to accomplish the best outcomes.

Conclusion

To join the influential club of good leaders, you need to focus on outcomes and on what needs to be accomplished by you and your team. A leader is not necessarily the one who has held a dominant position in a firm. A leader must have all these traits to focus on the needs of the company and the condition. On top of this, a natural-born leader focuses on strengths and has the natural force to mentor, inspire, and guide other people to set an excellent example for others to follow. Not everyone is or can be a natural-born leader. Your capability as a leader to call the shots and make sure that everyone is focused on the most critical use of their time are necessary traits, and, if applied correctly, can yield positive outcomes. You can strive to stand out in the world of leadership because the sky is no longer your limit, but your point of view...SO, let's all RISE TO GREATER HEIGHTS.

References

Dr. Real N, Kunene. "Rise to Greater Heights." 03 May 2020. <https://www.risetogreaterheights.com>

Kathryn Whittington

CEO of Boss Style LLC

https://www.linkedin.com/in/kathryn-whittington-21804a42
https://www.facebook.com/kathryn.whittington.75
https://www.instagram.com/vote_kathryn_whittington/

Kathryn Whittington is the Owner of Boss Style LLC and an Elected Official. Kathryn created Boss Style LLC for her granddaughters, to teach them about entrepreneurship and guide others on their journey to becoming effective leaders. Kathryn continues to speak across the country, where she shares insights on personal growth and empowerment. Kathryn is also a best-selling author, having co-authored several books and short stories. Commissioner Whittington was elected to serve on the Ashtabula County Board of Commissioners on January 3, 2017, for a four-year term of office. Following her initial term, Commissioner Whittington was re-elected to serve an additional four-year term, which began on January 3, 2021.Since her election, Kathryn has been deeply involved in addressing the drug epidemic at the local, statewide, and national levels. She spearheaded the Rural America initiative, advocating for prevention and collaboration, while highlighting the successes of Ashtabula County in combating drug addiction. With law enforcement being one of Kathryn's priorities,

Kathryn played a pivotal role in establishing the Crime Enforcement Agency of Ashtabula County (CEAAC).   With over 25 years of experience in community engagement and family support, she previously held roles such as Community Service Coordinator for the Ashtabula County Children Services Board, former Chair of the One Ohio Foundation Board, and served as the Interim Executive Director of the One Ohio Foundation Board. Currently, Kathryn participates in various Health & Human Services Committees through the County Commissioners Association of Ohio and the National Association of Counties, demonstrating her commitment to advancing public welfare.

FROM THE ASHES

By Kathryn Whittington

In the tapestry of life, some threads are woven with challenges, adversities, and unexpected turns. I never aspired to be a writer; my dream was simpler yet profound—to serve others. Today, I share my story as a testament to resilience, leadership, and unwavering hope. This narrative is not just mine; it's a beacon for those who may feel alone, a source of inspiration for realizing lifelong dreams, a call to make a difference in our communities, and to be the leader that you see yourself as.

My journey is intertwined with my faith, identity as a Christian, a wife, a mom, a nana, a public servant, a speaker, a presenter, and an advocate for children and families. My faith has been a constant stability in my life when other things were not. I knew very young that I was called upon to serve others. Serving was something that came very easily for me. I worked hard to make sure that I served others in a manner that God sent me here to do. When it came time for a career, social services chose me. Yes, that is correct, it chose me. My degrees are actually in Business Administration, Management, and Finance. The positions I applied for were always focused on children and families in need. So, I embarked on a social service career that has spanned over 25 years and has been driven by my faith and love for Christ.

Raised in the Methodist faith, my spiritual foundation became my rock when the world seemed uncertain. My faith journey has been a steadfast anchor in the tumultuous sea of life's uncertainties. It is a source of strength that has been pivotal in overcoming adversities and celebrating triumphs. In these pages, I share not just my story, but also the profound role that faith has played in my life and the successes it has ushered in, defining me as the leader I have become.

Motherhood, with its blessings and heartbreaks, has been a central theme in my life. As a mom and step-mom to five children, the challenges of raising a family became even more pronounced when addiction cast its shadow. Raising three granddaughters, a responsibility thrust upon me by unforeseen circumstances has become a reminder of the profound impact addiction can have on both the individual and the entire family.

The harsh reality of the national drug epidemic really hit home in 2013 when my house was burglarized. It was a night that marked not just the loss of material possessions but also a profound awakening to the harsh realities of addiction. The intrusion, born out of desperation, left me grappling with the aftermath and fueled a personal commitment to addressing addiction in our community and nationwide.

Having witnessed firsthand the destructive force of addiction, my life took on a new purpose. The burglary, a pivotal moment in my life, propelled me further into the realm of advocacy. Determined to be a voice for those affected by addiction, I embarked on a journey as a speaker and presenter at various drug epidemic forums. My presentation, "Rural America…Tackling the Drug Epidemic," born out of my experiences, underscores the power of partnerships and local efforts in combatting the pervasive drug epidemic afflicting communities nationwide. It seeks to shed light on the impact of addiction and emphasizes the role of partnerships and local efforts in combating this pervasive issue. It is my hope that sharing my story ignites a spark in others to join the fight against addiction.

The intimate encounter with addiction within my own family sparked a personal mission to support others facing this insidious disease. As a speaker and presenter at various drug epidemic forums, I passionately share my story, emphasizing the crucial role of partnerships and local efforts in combating the drug epidemic. Through my presentation,

"Rural America…Tackling the Drug Epidemic," I seek to inspire others to get involved, foster hope and resilience in the face of adversity, and let those know, you are not alone.

In the historically male-dominated realm of corporate leadership, the emergence of women CEOs, Executives, and Leaders represents a significant shift in the dynamics of power and influence. Being a woman in these roles transcends mere statistics; it embodies a paradigm shift in leadership styles, organizational cultures, and societal norms.

This journey of advocacy, partnership building, and legislative involvement serves as a testament to the transformative power of my commitment to my community. By actively participating in state and national dialogues, Ashtabula County has seen tangible improvements, and this is only the beginning. As a woman dedicated to positive change, I am fueled by the belief, that collective action can reshape the narrative and elevate the lives of those we serve.

Though I have never considered myself a CEO, as an elected official overseeing a county, I am that CEO. A woman CEO, Executive, and leader transcends individual achievements; it represents a transformative power that reshapes organizational cultures, societal norms, and the very definition of leadership. As women continue to ascend to the highest echelons of corporate leadership, their impact reverberates far beyond boardrooms, inspiring generations to come and forging a more inclusive and equitable future.

I have time and time again been afforded the opportunities to take an idea, bring community stakeholders to the table, and leave that table with a plan to execute serving our community and its needs.

For me, success is the positive difference in my actions and decisions made in Ashtabula County. As the largest county geographically in Ohio, our challenges were met with collaborative efforts. I spearheaded the creation of a dedicated drug task force, reflecting my commitment to fostering community growth and resilience under my dedicated leadership.

From the towering peaks of visionary leadership to the intricate labyrinths of ethical conduct, we have explored the vast landscape of leadership with curiosity and introspection.

At its core, leadership is not merely a position of authority or a title bestowed upon individuals; instead, it is a profound responsibility to inspire, guide, and empower others towards a common purpose. Throughout history, great leaders have emerged not solely through their actions but through their unwavering commitment to their values, people, and vision.

Leadership is a journey of continuous growth and learning. The path to effective leadership is paved with self-awareness, humility, and a relentless pursuit of personal and professional development. Leaders must recognize that growth is not a destination but a lifelong journey, characterized by a commitment to self-reflection and improvement. By cultivating self-awareness, leaders gain deeper insights into their strengths, weaknesses, and blind spots, enabling them to lead with authenticity and integrity. Additionally, humility serves as a cornerstone of effective leadership, reminding leaders of their fallibility and the importance of seeking guidance and feedback from others. Leaders must be open to feedback, embracing it as a catalyst for growth rather than viewing it as criticism. Furthermore, leaders must remain adaptable in the face of change, navigating uncertainty with resilience and flexibility. In a world characterized by rapid technological advancements and shifting socio-economic landscapes, leaders who embrace change as an opportunity rather than a threat are better equipped to lead their teams and organizations towards success. Embracing new perspectives, challenging assumptions, and embracing diversity of thought are essential components of effective leadership in an ever-evolving world.

Authentic leadership springs forth from a deep sense of purpose and integrity. Leaders who lead with authenticity are not merely driven by external recognition or power but are guided by an unwavering commitment to their core values and principles. They understand that authenticity is the foundation upon which trust and credibility are built. Authentic leaders act with transparency and honesty, communicating openly with their team members and stakeholders. By sharing their vision, goals, and challenges openly, they foster an environment of trust and mutual respect. Moreover, authentic leaders prioritize integrity in all their actions, consistently aligning their behaviors with their values and ethical standards. They lead by example, demonstrating integrity in even the most challenging circumstances, and holding themselves accountable for their decisions and actions. By embodying authenticity, transparency, and integrity, leaders inspire loyalty, commitment, and dedication among their followers, creating a culture of excellence and accountability within their organizations.

Effective leadership is inclusive and empathetic. Leaders who cultivate diverse and inclusive environments recognize the inherent value of every individual and actively seek to create spaces where all voices are heard and respected. By embracing diversity in its many forms - including but not limited to race, gender, ethnicity, age, sexual orientation, and socio-economic background - leaders foster a culture of belonging where everyone feels valued and empowered to contribute their unique perspectives and talents. Inclusive leaders understand that diversity is not only a moral imperative but also a strategic advantage, as diverse teams are more creative, innovative, and resilient in the face of challenges. Moreover, effective leaders demonstrate empathy by seeking to understand and empathize with the experiences, emotions, and perspectives of others. By practicing active listening, showing compassion, and being attuned to the needs and concerns of their team members, leaders build trust and rapport, fostering strong bonds and inspiring collective action. Empathetic leaders recognize that empathy is not a sign of weakness but rather a strength that enables them to connect with others on a deeper level, build meaningful relationships, and drive positive change within their organizations and communities. By cultivating inclusivity and empathy, leaders create environments where diversity thrives, innovation flourishes, and collaboration thrives, ultimately driving sustainable growth and success.

Leadership is not a solitary endeavor but a collaborative effort. Great leaders understand that the strength of their leadership lies not only in their capabilities but also in their ability to harness the collective talents and strengths of their team. They recognize that no one person has all the answers and that true innovation and progress emerge from diverse perspectives and collaborative efforts. Therefore, they prioritize building strong relationships based on trust, respect, and mutual support. By fostering a culture of collaboration, great leaders create environments where team members feel empowered to share their ideas, take initiative, and work together towards common goals. They encourage open communication, active participation, and constructive feedback, creating space for creativity and innovation to flourish. Moreover, great leaders empower their teams by providing them with the resources, autonomy, and support they need to succeed. They delegate authority, encourage risk-taking, and celebrate both individual and collective achievements, fostering a sense of ownership and accountability among team members. By empowering their teams, great leaders not only unlock their full potential but also cultivate a sense of pride, loyalty, and commitment, driving high performance and organizational success. In essence, great leaders understand that collaboration is not just a means to an end but a fundamental value that underpins their leadership philosophy, guiding their actions and decisions as they work together with their teams to achieve shared objectives.

Leadership is about making a positive impact on the world around us. Whether leading a team, an organization, or a community, leaders possess a unique opportunity and responsibility to leverage their influence for the greater good. They understand that leadership is not merely about achieving personal success or advancing individual interests but about serving a higher purpose and contributing to the betterment of society. Great leaders are driven by a sense of altruism and a desire to leave a lasting legacy of inspiration and innovation. They recognize that their actions and decisions have far-reaching consequences, not only for their immediate surroundings but also for future generations. Therefore, they strive to lead with integrity, empathy, and compassion, making decisions that prioritize the well-being of others and the planet. Whether implementing sustainable business practices, championing social justice initiatives, or spearheading community development projects, leaders are catalysts for positive change, driving meaningful progress and leaving indelible marks on the world. Moreover, great leaders understand that their impact extends beyond their immediate sphere of influence. They inspire and empower others to become leaders in their own right, fostering a legacy of leadership that transcends generations. By nurturing the next generation of change-makers and instilling in them the values of empathy, integrity, and service, leaders ensure that their impact endures long after they're gone. In essence, leadership is not just about achieving success for oneself but about leaving the world a better place than we found it, one act of leadership at a time.

Leading change is a complex but essential aspect of leadership, especially in dynamic environments. Successfully guiding a team or organization through change requires strategic planning, effective communication, and strong leadership skills. Here are key principles and strategies for leading change:

- Define a Compelling Vision: Articulate a clear and inspiring vision for change, emphasizing its alignment with organizational objectives and the benefits it brings.

- Foster Transparent Communication: Develop a robust communication plan, ensuring transparency and consistency to keep everyone informed, address concerns promptly, and celebrate milestones together.

- Cultivate Supportive Coalitions: Identify and engage key stakeholders, harnessing their influence to champion change and garner broader support across the organization.

- Ignite Urgency: Communicate the imperative for change, emphasizing the risks of inertia and the opportunities that change presents, to instill a sense of urgency among stakeholders.

- Empower Employee Engagement: Involve employees at all levels, encouraging their active participation, soliciting feedback, and integrating their insights into the change process.

- Provide Adequate Resources: Allocate necessary resources—financial, technological, and human—to facilitate the change, and offer training and support to ensure successful adaptation.

- Address Resistance Proactively: Anticipate and address resistance by empathetically listening to concerns, providing information, and involving detractors in decision-making.

- Celebrate Progress: Recognize and celebrate incremental achievements to maintain morale and reinforce positive behaviors that drive change.

- Empower Change Agents: Identify and empower change champions within the organization, enabling them to influence peers positively and drive change from within.

- Offer Clear Guidance: Provide a structured roadmap for change, breaking down tasks into manageable steps and clarifying each individual's role in achieving the overarching objectives.

- Adapt with Agility: Remain flexible and responsive to evolving circumstances, adjusting the change strategy, as needed, based on feedback and unforeseen challenges.

- Lead by Example: Demonstrate unwavering commitment to change by embodying desired behaviors and actively supporting the transformation process.

- Cultivate Innovation: Encourage a culture of innovation, inspiring employees to explore new ideas and approaches that align with the change vision.

- Foster Supportive Environment: Create a psychologically safe environment where individuals feel comfortable expressing concerns and seeking assistance as they navigate change.

- Measure Progress: Establish measurable goals and track progress using key performance indicators to ensure the change effort stays on course and delivers desired outcomes.

- Provide Feedback and Recognition: Offer constructive feedback and recognize contributions to foster a culture of continuous improvement and appreciation.

- Learn from Experience: Conduct regular reviews to reflect on successes, challenges, and areas for improvement, leveraging insights to enhance future change initiatives.

- Institutionalize Change: Embed the changes into the organizational culture, reinforcing new behaviors and norms until they become ingrained in daily operations.

- Anticipate Challenges: Proactively identify potential setbacks and develop contingency plans to mitigate risks and maintain momentum during the change process.

- Celebrate Completion: Acknowledge the successful completion of the change effort and celebrate the organization's resilience and adaptability in navigating transformation.

Driven by a deep-seated desire to witness positive change and growth in my home county, I made the bold decision to run for the office of Ashtabula County Commissioner. When my journey began, I knew that my faith would carry me through no matter what happened. What I was not prepared for was that during my campaign my faith was questioned and challenged by others. I had never encountered this before. I found myself wanting to take and protect what I believed in.

It was clear to me that our collective voice was not resonating as it should. Once elected, I realized that being actively engaged in my community was not enough; I needed to extend my reach to the state and federal levels. Eager to establish myself and make a meaningful impact, I grappled with the nuances of leadership. The challenges of being a female elected official were stark, requiring me to establish myself, earn respect, and hone my leadership skills. Recognizing my need for growth, I sought guidance and mentorship from fellow women leaders, participated in leadership programs, and emerged ready to chart a new course in my political leadership to navigate the complexities of my position.

Having spent time at Children Services, I had already established connections with many local liaisons. Building on these relationships,

I began to expand my network. Elevating my advocacy, I became actively involved at the state and federal levels through committees at the County Commissioners Association of Ohio and the National Association of Counties. I understood that building partnerships is not confined to the local arena; it extends to statewide and national levels. The impact of such collaborations can be directly felt at the grassroots level. This is how active involvement and cultivated relationships at the state and national levels have directly influenced positive change in Ashtabula County.

My commitment to human services, children services, and criminal justice advocacy led to significant contributions at both the local and state levels. In the realm of advocacy, being appointed to boards is not just beneficial; it's essential. It ensures that our county has a seat at the table and a voice that demands to be heard. As I navigate challenges unique to Ashtabula County, I draw upon my abilities to bring people together for the greater good and extend my leadership skills beyond the confines of traditional governances, reflecting a commitment to the holistic well-being of my community.

A big part of my leadership *experience* or *journey* is serving as a County Commissioner. As a commissioner this is the most frequently asked question - what do you do? I would like to share with all of you what the responsibilities of a County Commissioner are.

The Board of Commissioners consists of three commissioners elected by county residents. Two commissioners are elected in the presidential year and one is elected in the gubernatorial year. Commissioners serve a four-year term, and there is no limit on the number of terms they can serve.

County Commissioners have specific and limited authority governed by state legislation. The main focus of the commissioners is that we are the Budget and Appropriating Authority for the County. We adopt the

County Budget annually, appropriating funds to many departments and elected county officials, keeping revenues and expenditures in line to maintain a balanced budget.

As a member of the Board, I levy taxes for county purposes, issue bonds for capital improvements, and serve as the purchasing and contracting agent for the County, along with the other two Commissioners.

We have direct authority over the following departments:

- Building Department
- Commissioners Office
- Community Services and Planning
- Dog Warden
- Emergency Management/911
- Environmental Services
- Lodging Tax
- Maintenance and Risk Management
- Ashtabula County Department of Job and Family Services
- Ashtabula County Nursing and Rehabilitation Center
- Geneva Lodge and Conference Center

As a Commissioner we appoint a full-time Clerk whose duties are to keep a record of all transactions of the Board, to be the custodian of all the records and proceedings of the Board, and to act as the official witness to all legislative actions taken by the Commissioners. We also appoint an Administrator who oversees the operations of all departments under the control and jurisdiction of the Board and advises us on the financial condition of the County.

We appoint board members to various organizations throughout Ashtabula County. Among our many other duties, we serve in some capacity on over 35 local boards and commissions and various state and national committees.

The Board of Commissioners works closely with the County Auditor and Treasurer. The Auditor serves as the County Chief Fiscal Officer. The Treasurer serves as the County Chief Investment Officer.

We work closely with and are responsible for appropriating money to fund operations for the following elected officials:

- Sheriff
- Coroner
- Prosecuting Attorney
- the Courts
- Clerk of Courts
- Recorder
- Auditor

There is one huge difference between conducting private and public business. Public means exactly what it says, which I do not disagree with. I believe in transparency, as tax dollars fund my position as a Commissioner.

To explain a little about how boards work, no decisions are made alone. You must have what is referred to as a "quorum." Most of the meetings, deliberations, and decisions must be in a public meeting, with notice going out to the public at a minimum of 24 hours before the meeting begins. Board Member expectations and responsibilities are not to be taken lightly. I am required to make decisions regarding programs, policies, procedures, expenditures, budgets, hiring, and termination of employees. I am called upon to work with other elected officials, community leaders, and outside agencies, always with the mindset of serving the constituents of my county.

The Board of Commissioners is required to conduct 50 meetings per year as regular meetings, with special meetings being allowed with 24 public notice. We generally hold these sessions on Tuesdays at 1:00

p.m. in our Commissioners Conference Room, but on the 4th Tuesday of each month (before Covid 19) hold an evening session in various locations throughout Ashtabula County. We hold numerous work sessions to discuss county business and make decisions. These sessions and meetings are open to the public and they are encouraged to attend.

I had to learn a whole lot about the Ohio Sunshine Laws and what my role as a Commissioner really was. So many rules!

So, now that we got through the official part of being a commissioner, let's talk about the other part of being an elected official. Events, events, and more events.

As an elected official, I am invited to events, ribbon cuttings, parades, and dedications. We are asked to volunteer and help with local fundraisers for different organizations and be guest speakers. The Commissioners issue proclamations for successes, milestones, and retirements, honoring and acknowledging these special times in the lives of our constituents.

These events all support the residents and the community that as an elected official you represent. It is worth it all.

Being an elected official, allows me to tell the story from a different perspective than most. I have met those individuals who do not know how they will get through the day, let alone where the next meal, shelter, clothing, and basic hygiene items will come from. I have volunteered my time throughout my lifetime to allow my hands to be the physical tools, doing God's work, through me.

Leading change is a perpetual journey demanding resilience, flexibility, and a dedication to perpetual enhancement. By integrating these principles and tactics, leaders adeptly maneuver through the intricacies of change, steering their teams towards triumphant and enduring transformation.

Through the application of these principles and tactics, both individuals and organizations adeptly navigate change, fostering an environment that embraces positivity and adaptability while championing continuous advancement and expansion. Effective change management hinges on a commitment to communication, collaboration, and ongoing learning.

Effective leaders recognize the importance of continuous learning and development as indispensable elements of their leadership journey. Commitment to staying current with industry trends, actively seeking feedback, and embracing a growth mindset are foundational to sustained leadership excellence. Leaders who prioritize ongoing learning exhibit a proactive approach to understanding the evolving landscape of their industry, ensuring that their strategies remain relevant and forward-thinking. Actively seeking feedback demonstrates a humility that allows leaders to refine their skills and address areas for improvement. Embracing a growth mindset fosters an environment of innovation and adaptability, encouraging both personal and organizational development. In essence, effective leaders understand that learning is a lifelong journey, and their dedication to self-improvement contributes significantly to their sustained success and the overall growth of their teams and organizations.

- Setting Clear Goals: Identifies specific areas for enhancement, be it refining leadership capabilities, improving communication skills, or broadening her knowledge base.

- Seeking Feedback: Recognizing the value of feedback, she actively solicits input from mentors, colleagues, and team members to pinpoint areas needing improvement and gain diverse perspectives.

- Continuous Learning: Prioritizes ongoing education, actively pursuing opportunities for professional development such as workshops, courses, conferences, and relevant literature.

- Embracing Challenges: Rather than avoiding challenges, view them as avenues for growth. Willingly take on new responsibilities and ventures that push you beyond your comfort zone.

- Building a Support Network: Surrounding yourself with a supportive network of peers, mentors, and coaches is crucial for providing encouragement, guidance, and accountability as you progress towards your objectives.

- Reflection and Adaptation: Regular self-reflection allows you to gauge your advancement, acknowledge achievements, and learn from setbacks. Adjust your strategies as necessary, remaining adaptable and resilient in the face of obstacles.

- Mindfulness and Well-being: Acknowledge the significance of self-care and well-being in sustaining peak performance. Practices like mindfulness, physical exercise, and maintaining work-life balance are integral aspects of your self-improvement journey.

- Leading by Example: Most importantly, set a precedent by actively demonstrating your commitment to self-improvement. By doing so, hopefully, inspire others to invest in their own growth and development.

Continuously seeking opportunities to enhance my leadership skills is a top priority. I've engaged in programs such as the JoAnn Davidson Leadership Institute, The NACo Professional Development Academy, and the NACo Leadership Institute. I firmly believe that ongoing development is indispensable for being at the forefront of effective leadership and is key to self-improvement.

Now, let's talk about self-awareness and how that contributes to being a successful leader. Here are some of my views and what I practice.

Self-awareness is the capacity to recognize and understand one's thoughts, feelings, behaviors, strengths, weaknesses, values, and motivations. It entails a conscious awareness of personal identity, encompassing personality traits, beliefs, and the impact of actions on oneself and others. Serving as a foundational element of emotional intelligence and personal development, self-awareness involves various key aspects.

Emotional self-awareness entails recognizing and understanding one's own emotions, identifying their origins, and acknowledging their influence on thoughts and behaviors. Understanding personal values and beliefs involves being conscious of the principles guiding decision-making. Self-aware individuals acknowledge their strengths and areas for improvement, conducting an honest assessment of skills and talents. Understanding personality traits, such as introversion or extroversion, openness, and conscientiousness, is crucial for recognizing how these traits influence interactions with others. Self-aware individuals also recognize the impact of their words and actions on those around them, attuned to the dynamics of relationships and the consequences of their behavior.

Self-reflection, a deliberate and conscious consideration of one's experiences, actions, and thoughts, is integral to self-awareness. It involves examining beliefs, values, and behaviors with a critical and curious mindset, providing insights into motivations, making sense of past experiences, and guiding future approaches. Key elements of self-reflection include thoughtful analysis, learning from experiences, assessing goal alignment, embracing continuous improvement, and enhancing decision-making by considering different perspectives and potential outcomes.

Self-reflection and self-awareness are interconnected, with engagement in self-reflection deepening understanding and leading to greater self-awareness. Both practices are integral to personal and professional development, empowering individuals to make intentional choices, comprehend motivations, and continually learn and grow. These practices contribute to improved decision-making, enhanced relationships, and a more fulfilling life.

Let's carry forth the wisdom and insights gained from our exploration into our own leadership journeys. May we all continue to strive for excellence, lead with compassion and integrity, and unleash the full potential of ourselves and those we have the privilege to lead.

As you inspire, empower, and lead, may your leadership journey be filled with purpose, passion, and profound impact.

For me, from the ashes of personal adversity rose a woman of strength, resilience, and leadership. Sharing my journey, I aim to ignite hope in others during their darkest moments, reminding them they are not alone, and empowering them to recognize the transformative power within each of us to effect change.

Donna J. Thomas

CEO of Mountainside Gals!!!
Entreprenuer, Speaker, Podcaster & International Best Selling Author

https://www.linkedin.com/in/donnacthomas/
https://www.facebook.com/SurvivoroftheStorms
https://www.instagram.com/mommadonnafromthemountainside/
https://linktr.ee/MountainsideGals
https://www.mountainsidegals.com

Donna J. Thomas, CEO of Mountainside Gals is an influencer among LuLaRoe retailers and has sustained sales among the top 10% of the company. Donna coaches and mentors her team and when she has free time, she appears as a guest on podcasts, is a podcaster, is a speaker, and is an international best seller author. She has built a sizeable active community of women who engage and uplift each other, and all share the love fashion. Career wise, Donna has had progressive leadership advancement and built programs for women to be mentored/coached and advanced through the ranks. Her leadership as well as mothering styles are strongly inspired by her life's faith journey. Donna challenges herself to go the extra mile in all that she does, and she aims to bless lives daily. She lives with her husband, son and nephew in the mountains of southern Frederick County, Maryland.

UNVEILING CORPORATE GAMESMANSHIP: LESSONS BEYOND THE BOARDROOM

By Donna J. Thomas

Introduction

As I reflect on a career spanning over three decades in the intricate landscape of corporate America, I've garnered invaluable insights into the subtle nuances of navigating its dynamic terrain. While Betty Harragan's seminal work, *Games Mother Never Taught You: Corporate Gamesmanship for Women*, lays a solid foundation, my personal journey has unearthed additional layers of wisdom. Join me as we delve into the strategies and principles that have shaped my approach to corporate success.

My Personal Journey

Having held the CEO title in my small business and climbed the corporate ladder in corporate America, with my last title being Vice President, I've accumulated a wealth of experience. Among other responsibilities, I built a personal and professional development group for women to help them climb the ranks in leadership and become directors or vice presidents.

Wisdom and Advice From My Personal Journey

Corporate gamesmanship refers to the strategic and sometimes competitive maneuvers, tactics, or behaviors employed within a corporate environment to achieve certain objectives. These can include actions taken by individuals or groups to gain advantage, influence outcomes, or navigate complex organizational dynamics. Corporate gamesmanship often involves aspects of negotiation, persuasion, networking, and sometimes even manipulation to achieve desired results, whether it's securing a promotion, winning a deal, or outmaneuvering competitors. It's about understanding the rules of the corporate landscape and leveraging them to one's advantage, sometimes through subtle or indirect means.

Many pieces of wisdom and advice come to mind, but those documented here are the ones that I consider critical—some may register as common sense, but others are not easy. I have to tell you that looking back over my years in leadership, I find that these were in play from the beginning and they have sustained me over time.

Gratitude: The Pillar of Resilience

Cultivating a Grateful Mindset

Gratitude isn't merely a pleasant sentiment; it's a potent force that anchors us amidst the ebbs and flows of professional life. Through daily practices like meditation, prayer, and journaling, we can cultivate a resilient spirit that enables us to navigate challenges with grace and determination. Our gratitude list serves to remind us of what is important and why we are doing what we do.

Navigating the Competitive Landscape

In a world where competition often reigns supreme, sincerity and diligence serve as our most potent weapons. By meticulously documenting our journey and presenting well-researched facts, we not only command respect from our peers but also foster alliances rooted in collaboration rather than cutthroat competition.

Gratitude helps with the work ethic required to reach collective success. This is essential to navigating the competitive landscape.

A Journey Shaped by Gratitude

My upbringing, marked by humble beginnings and scarcity, instilled in me a deep-seated sense of gratitude. These early experiences laid the groundwork for a career marked by acknowledgment and appreciation, guiding my interactions with colleagues and superiors alike.

Work-Life Balance:

I would not be doing anyone justice without mentioning this. Work hours can be excessive at times, but you need to "balance" that with a growing family. The time you are away from the kids is time that is never returned. For example, I gave up a keynote speaking engagement for my daughter's fifth grade graduation. I believe it was the best decision ever and I have no regrets. Did it cost me professionally in the long run? If it did, I never knew. I was so busy and in high demand for all kinds of things so if there was any flack, it was in the "noise," and I never noticed.

The key to achieving this without guilt is to have a plan and a schedule that you can stick to and to have the flexibility and adaptability to work with it so that you don't miss key family events and still complete your projects on time. The people who are in your life—ie. a spouse—can also work and be supportive, so if you have child or children, one of you can show support.

When you take on the challenge of climbing the corporate ladder, you should first determine what your non-negotiables are—and work out a plan so you never compromise on them. You should have a great communication line with the boss so that they can support you.

If you don't have a child or children but you have other obligations, this work-life balance is also very important. Examples may include, but not be limited to, caring for a parent or grandparent, signing in an international gospel group, a book club, an exercise class, a bible study, a leadership position in a nonprofit (part-time), etc. Whatever the obligations are, always have a plan to "cover" or an acceptable plan in place to fulfill those obligations. NOTE: this can also apply to parents, but complicates the Work-Life Balance.

If you have no obligations, make sure you don't work long hours and not play. You need to "detox" from work and take care of you. Work-life balance could be making time for a massage, a new hair-do, shopping, getting the nails done, hanging with friends, or going to a sound bath.

Integrity: The North Star of Leadership

Upholding Ethical Standards

Integrity isn't just a virtue; it's a guiding principle that steers us through ethical dilemmas. Upholding honesty and transparency, even in the absence of supervision, lays the foundation for enduring trust and credibility. This is a very important principle for climbing the corporate ladder. Integrity is tightly aligned with trust.

The Essence of Ethical Leadership

Leadership devoid of integrity is a hollow facade. By prioritizing diligence and thoroughness in every task, we set a standard for ethical leadership that inspires trust and respect among our peers and superiors alike.

The Cost of Compromised Values

In the pursuit of expediency, it can be tempting to cut corners and compromise our values. However, the long-term consequences of such actions far outweigh any short-term gains. Each decision we make becomes a reflection of our character, shaping our reputation in the eyes of others.

Use this judiciously. If you are running out of time to draw a chart electronically, draw it by hand. Still, making the meeting on time and delivering the same message is most powerful. We can be creative in its delivery.

Generosity: Fostering a Culture of Abundance

Embracing a Culture of Giving

Generosity isn't just about material wealth; it's about investing time, recognition, and empathy in those around us. By striking a balance between professional rigor and opportunities for camaraderie and celebration, we foster a workplace culture anchored in mutual support.

The Power of Empathetic Leadership

Accessible and empathetic leadership transcends hierarchical boundaries. By actively listening to the concerns of our team members and expressing genuine gratitude for their contributions, we cultivate a sense of belonging and loyalty that drives collective success.

An ounce of kindness is worth its weight in gold and being an active listener will yield great rewards for you, your team and superiors.

Serving Others: The Heartbeat of Leadership

Leading by Serving

True leadership isn't about authority; it's about service. By prioritizing the needs of our team members and empowering them to succeed, we foster a culture of collaboration and mutual respect that propels us toward our shared goals.

Drawing Inspiration from Exemplary Leaders

Exemplary leaders, like Abraham Lincoln, lead not with brute force but with humility and empathy. By embracing these principles, we not only become more effective leaders but also leave a lasting legacy of positive change that inspires those around us.

Reputation: The Currency of Influence

Cultivating a Resilient Reputation

In the ever-changing landscape of corporate dynamics, our reputation precedes us. By consistently delivering results, even in the face of adversity, we build trust and credibility that open doors to new opportunities and propel us toward our professional goals.

Pioneering Transformative Initiatives

Bold initiatives require more than just vision; they demand resilience and resourcefulness. By leveraging our expertise and strategic acumen, we can spearhead transformative projects that redefine organizational paradigms and drive sustainable growth.

I have a wealth of collective experiences that have grown me to be a thankful spirit, and being a thankful spirit has helped me focus on developing a reputation of being able to get anything done, especially the hard things. I've had a few jobs throughout my career, and I can only think of two times when I had to use a resume. The responsibilities and opportunities afforded to me have been mostly attributed to my reputation of being able to get things done, no matter how hard the task. In fact, I have stepped into larger positions of responsibility, taking on tasks that peers firmly believed were impossible to achieve. Success was achieved by getting in front of a huge transitional project that needed clarity, organization, resourcefulness, communication, and routine reporting of progress. I leveraged tools to build excitement and to encourage adoption and participation in the changes to the group. Each of these experiences, in my humble opinion, is a plum project.

Accepting a plum project was my favorite task. Over time, leaders and bosses would get out of my way and pretty much approve the budget and resources that I considered necessary to make the project a reality. Many of these projects ended up significantly improving ROI and profit margins and/or growing new profitable lines of business to the point at which substantial bonuses and stock options were gifted.

Throughout my career, examples of plum projects included the success of Y2K in finance and payroll, achieving a special certification to gain new market entry (to win new business), and achieving compliance to meet stiff government regulation in the areas of Sarbanes-Oxley, safety, quality, health (HIPAA), insurance, traffic, cybersecurity, security, and internal audit. Some of these plum projects included not only reaching the end but also transforming change in the organization by adopting new procedures and processes and migrating from one set of practices to another. This also included multifaceted configuration management of documents, hardware, software, procedures, processes, and customer deliverables including business development and marketing activity.

Navigating Complex Terrain

From navigating regulatory compliance to spearheading organizational restructuring, adept project management is indispensable. By successfully navigating these challenges, we not only enhance our reputation but also position ourselves as catalysts for organizational growth and innovation.

A benefit of this experience is that my next assignment came from the reputation I built, not from looking at my resume or even asking for my resume.

Advancement in Career: Celebrating Milestones

Embracing Triumphs and Tribulations

Each milestone in our career journey is a testament to our resilience and tenacity. By celebrating these victories, no matter how small, we reaffirm our commitment to personal and professional growth, inspiring those around us to reach for new heights.

Pioneering New Frontiers

Stepping into uncharted territories requires courage and conviction. By embracing innovation and seizing opportunities, we can carve out new paths to success, defying conventional limitations and reshaping the future of our organizations.

Charting the Course Ahead

As I reflect on the chapters of my career, I'm reminded of the transformative power of perseverance and resilience. Each challenge surmounted, each triumph celebrated, has shaped me into the leader I am today, poised to inspire and empower others to embrace their own journeys of growth and discovery.

Conclusion

In the ever-evolving landscape of corporate gamesmanship, women emerge as architects of change, wielding gratitude, integrity, generosity, and servant leadership as their tools of empowerment. By cultivating transformative initiatives and nurturing resilient reputations, women can redefine the rules of the game, paving the way for a future generation of trailblazers.

Lynn M. Shallow

LMS Coaching Inc.
Money Breakthrough Business Coach

https://www.linkedin.com/in/lynn-shallow-080362300
https://realbizconfidence.com

Through her unique journey of continuous personal growth and professional experience, Lynn champions the empowerment of women who aspire to corporate leadership or as CEO of their own business by developing R.E.A.L. confidence as a key foundation for success. Lynn's resilience in the face of constant life changes and challenges has deeply shaped her perseverance and inner strength. Her commitment to continuous learning led her to more progressively responsible positions in her corporate career. Through her coaching business, she shares invaluable insights garnered from her journey in leading women to powerfully and effectively navigate their career or entrepreneurship paths with confidence. The foundational approach of R.E.A.L. confidence is crucial to foster inner confidence and readiness for succeeding in leadership roles. This proactive stance ensures stronger alignment between women's desire and preparedness in their business or their leadership career aspirations, benefiting both themselves and their business or the organizations they serve.

THE FORCE OF WOMEN CEOS: R.E.A.L. BIZ CONFIDENCE EMPOWERMENT

By Lynn M. Shallow

In today's corporate landscape, an obvious void remains: the lack of diverse voices at the forefront of decision-making. Picture a boardroom bustling with suits, where male voices dominate, often drowning out the few women trying to make themselves heard. This all-too-familiar scenario highlights the pressing need for authentic, confident female leaders!

Despite strides toward gender equality, women face persistent barriers on their path to the C-suite. Documented research underscores a widespread lack of confidence among even highly skilled and educated women, potentially contributing to the shortage of female leaders in top positions. Empowering women through the development of R.E.A.L. Biz Confidence—hereafter referred to as "real confidence"—rooted in inner strength and authenticity, presents a transformative solution for empowered decision-making and actions that bring about significant changes in women's professional lives so that they can break through the glass ceiling into a new level of success and achievement. This chapter focuses on the foundations of real confidence as it applies to female leadership development within the corporate context, while recognizing that they also apply to women who are CEOs of their own businesses, illustrating the universal applicability of these foundations across diverse professional settings.

In a corporate environment where women may not always find adequate support, many are increasingly transitioning to entrepreneurship, where they can chart their own course as CEOs and create success on their own terms. This trend not only reflects a response to institutional barriers but also highlights the significant cost to companies that fail to support women equipped in their pursuit of leadership roles. The loss of talent and the stifling of potential innovation represent missed opportunities that can have long-term consequences for companies striving to remain competitive in today's dynamic business environment.

Real confidence is not only about skills or education but about tapping into the untapped reservoirs of inner power to navigate the outer challenges. Real confidence serves as a catalyst for success amid these challenges by transcending surface-level approaches, rooted in foundational pillars that will be further explored. It stands as a beacon of empowerment, offering both companies and aspiring women leaders a transformative pathway to leadership development that cultivates a culture of inclusivity, innovation, and excellence.

For women aspiring to C-suite positions, real confidence can empower them to navigate leadership complexities with poise and purpose. Through a holistic approach encompassing self-awareness for aligned choices and by evolving confidence, skill development and mentorship, we can unlock our innate potential by breaking through glass ceilings and redefining corporate leadership boundaries. By embracing real confidence, we can harness the power to lead with conviction, compassion, and courage, navigating corporate complexities with resilience and authenticity.

Aspiring women leaders face many challenges on their journey to the C-suite, but real confidence serves as a steadfast guide, empowering them to effectively navigate these complexities. Through a multifaceted approach that encompasses self-awareness, skill development, and mentorship, women can cultivate the inner strength and clarity of purpose needed to overcome barriers and seize opportunities. Mentorship, in particular, plays a pivotal role, providing guidance, support, and invaluable insights from experienced leaders. By embracing real confidence and leveraging mentorship, we can also redefine corporate leadership boundaries, paving the way for a more inclusive and innovative future. As we lead more with conviction, compassion, and courage, we become beacons of inspiration for future generations, driving meaningful change within our companies and beyond.

In today's competitive landscape, embracing real confidence is not just an ethical imperative but also a strategic necessity for companies. By fostering environments that celebrate authenticity and empower diverse voices, companies unlock their workforce's full potential, driving innovation and sustainable growth. Actively promoting real confidence among women leaders not only enhances internal talent pipelines but also mitigates the risk of talent loss. This dual approach fosters a culture of inclusivity and empowerment, encouraging women to pursue leadership roles within the company. Such initiatives not only retain top talent but also positively impact societal norms and opportunities. By exploring the intersection of real confidence and women's leadership development, this chapter inspires an opportunity for transformative change, creating a more inclusive and equitable corporate landscape.

Join me in uncovering the journey toward unlocking the potential of empowered leadership through real confidence—a journey that sets the stage for lasting change. Let's begin by diving into the foundational elements of real confidence.

As women journey toward C-suite positions, they navigate an evolving landscape requiring adaptability and authenticity. Cultivating confidence, particularly through fostering real confidence, is paramount. Real confidence intertwines with energetic intelligence and leadership development, serving as an anchor that grounds the leadership journey in integrity. Energetic intelligence equips us with self-awareness and emotional agility, while leadership development empowers us to hone skills and amplify impact as transformative leaders in the corporate realm. As real confidence is cultivated, potential is unlocked, inspiring others, fostering innovation, and driving meaningful change within and beyond our organizations. Let's now delve into the foundational elements represented by the acronyms of R.E.A.L.

Realigned confidence is pivotal in the journey of leadership development, particularly for women. It offers a profound sense of self-awareness, emotional intelligence, and resilience, which are indispensable qualities for navigating the complexities of the corporate landscape. Unlike conventional confidence, which may rely solely on external validation or surface-level achievements, realigned confidence requires us to cultivate a deeper understanding of ourselves, our values, and our purpose. This type of confidence empowers us to adjust our approaches, perspectives, and goals in response to evolving circumstances, ensuring we remain true to ourselves while navigating the challenges of leadership.

Rooted confidence serves as a steadfast anchor, grounding us in our authenticity and guiding our leadership journey with integrity. It enables us to lead with conviction, compassion, and courage, inspiring not only us but also our teams to excel. It serves as a fundamental building block by providing a stable foundation upon which to navigate the complexities of the business world. Rooted confidence emanates from a deep understanding of our values, strengths, and capabilities, allowing us to authentically express ourselves and assert our leadership in various professional settings. This inner sense of self-assurance enables us to stay true to our authentic selves, even in the face of challenges or societal expectations. Rooted confidence also empowers us to cultivate resilience, adaptability, and a growth mindset, essential qualities for success in today's dynamic business environment. By grounding ourselves in our values and strengths, we can confidently pursue our goals, make bold decisions, and overcome obstacles with more grace and resilience. Fostering a sense of empowerment, rooted confidence enables us to advocate for ourselves, negotiate effectively, and seize opportunities for growth and advancement. Ultimately, rooted confidence enables us to achieve meaningful success in both our professional and personal lives.

Resilience is an indispensable component of real confidence for women, offering a sturdy foundation upon which to navigate the challenges and uncertainties of the business world. In the face of obstacles, setbacks, or discrimination, resilience enables us to bounce back with strength and determination, refusing to be deterred by adversity. This resilience is not merely about enduring difficulties but also about learning and growing from them, emerging stronger and more capable in the process. By cultivating resilience, we develop a deep sense of self-assurance and inner strength, allowing us to face challenges head-on and persevere in the pursuit of our goals. Resilience also fosters adaptability and flexibility. By embodying resilience, we are not easily shaken by setbacks or failures but instead view them as opportunities for growth and development. This mindset of resilience fuels real confidence, empowering us to lead by unleashing our inner power, harnessing our full potential, and achieving meaningful success in both our personal and our professional lives.

Evolving confidence is a dynamic force that plays a pivotal role in women achieving real confidence. Unlike a static attribute, evolving confidence recognizes that confidence levels are fluid, continually shaped by new experiences, challenges, and opportunities. As we navigate various situations and roles, our confidence evolves, reflecting our growing understanding of our strengths, abilities, and potential. Evolving confidence empowers us to embrace change, take risks, and seize opportunities for growth and advancement. It encourages us to recognize and leverage our own strengths, abilities, and potential to affect positive change, fostering a sense of ownership over our careers.

By embracing the concept of evolving confidence, we can cultivate a mindset of resilience, adaptability, and growth, essential qualities for embodying real confidence. Evolving confidence enables us to lead with authenticity, resilience, empathy, and a commitment to lifelong learning, ultimately equipping us to attain meaningful success across both our personal pursuits and professional endeavors.

Empowered confidence holds profound significance for us as we aspire to leadership positions as it offers a transformative approach that differs from conventional confidence. Unlike traditional notions of confidence that may rely solely on external validation or conformity to established norms, empowered confidence is deeply rooted in our values and self-assurance. It empowers us to embrace our authenticity and navigate the corporate landscape with resilience. As empowered women leaders, we advocate not only for ourselves but also for others, creating inclusive environments where everyone feels valued and empowered to contribute. When empowered, we are also better equipped to navigate challenges and seize opportunities for growth and advancement, both for ourselves and those we lead. In doing so, we pave the way for a more inclusive and equitable corporate landscape where all individuals can thrive based on their talents, skills, and merit.

Authentic confidence is essential and indispensable for women aspiring to leadership positions, offering a distinctive approach that sets them apart from conventional confidence norms. Unlike traditional confidence, which may prioritize outward presentation or conformity to societal expectations, authentic confidence is deeply rooted in our values and self-assurance. It empowers us to navigate the corporate landscape with authenticity and resilience, essential qualities for effective leadership. This genuine confidence goes beyond surface-level traits, emphasizing our inner strength and self-awareness. Authenticity entails aligning our actions with our values, beliefs, and identity, allowing us to lead with integrity, transparency, and humility. By embracing our uniqueness and vulnerabilities, we foster genuine connections and cultivate a culture of openness and collaboration within our organization without oversharing or being an open book!

Assertiveness plays a crucial role in expressing ourselves authentically and confidently, whether in personal or professional contexts. Assertive leaders demonstrate the courage to advocate for their ideas and needs, create and assert healthier boundaries when necessary, and make decisive decisions with confidence. By leading with authenticity and assertiveness, we can drive progress and achieve goals while inspiring trust and respect from our teams and colleagues. For example, openly sharing our challenges and failures during team meetings demonstrates transparency, honesty, and vulnerability, fostering a culture of trust and openness. This authenticity builds strong relationships, enhances employee engagement and trust, and fosters a sense of belonging, ultimately leading to higher levels of productivity and performance. By embracing assertiveness, we take control of our professional interactions, enabling us to navigate challenges with grace and integrity, and ultimately leading to greater fulfillment and success in both personal and professional endeavors.

Liberated confidence also offers a transformative approach that distinguishes itself from conventional confidence norms. Unlike traditional confidence, which may be confined by self-imposed limitations and societal expectations, liberated confidence empowers us to navigate the corporate landscape with authenticity and resilience, essential attributes for effective leadership. Liberated confidence is particularly vital for us in our leadership roles. In many professional settings, we face unique challenges and barriers that can undermine our confidence and hinder our advancement. Liberated confidence allows us to break free from these constraints, enabling us to embrace our authentic selves fully and assert our leadership with courage and conviction. Liberated confidence also enables us to transcend perceived boundaries and pursue ambitious goals with unwavering determination. Liberated from constraints, our journey becomes a continuous cycle of learning, characterized by personal and professional growth. As women leaders, by transcending societal expectations and embracing our true strengths and values, we can inspire others, challenge the status quo, and drive positive change within our organization. Liberated confidence empowers us to lead with authenticity, paving the way for greater diversity, inclusivity, and innovation in leadership.

Leadership confidence, while not a widely recognized term in psychology or leadership studies, refers to a combination of self-assurance, belief in one's leadership abilities, and the ability to inspire confidence in others. It encompasses the confidence to make decisions, take risks, communicate effectively, and guide others toward common goals. By embracing our liberated and assertive selves, we as leaders can fearlessly navigate challenges, make difficult decisions, and take calculated risks to drive progress within our organization.

To summarize, real confidence equips us with the tools to navigate the intricate corporate terrain with courage, resilience, authenticity, and a dedication to continuous growth. By embracing these foundational pillars, we can foster a robust sense of self-assurance, lead with confidence and integrity, and catalyze positive transformation within our organization and broader communities. Let's now take a look at how we can cultivate real confidence.

While it's important to acknowledge the persistent gender gaps that exist within companies, cultivating real confidence requires us to recognize that true empowerment begins from within. It's about nurturing our inner confidence to pave the way for outer success. With this understanding, we will explore the key aspects that empower us to responsibly unleash our inner power to effectively lead our organization. Please note that while the following aspects contribute to both our inner and outer power to varying degrees, some may involve more tangible actions or behaviors, while others may involve more internal shifts in mindset and perspective. For example, self-discipline involves the practice of managing one's time, energy, and resources, which is a behavior that can lead to both inner growth and tangible achievements. Similarly, continuous learning involves actively seeking opportunities for personal and professional development, which contributes to both internal growth and external success in terms of acquiring new skills and knowledge.

As we embark on our journey through an ever-evolving landscape, self-reflection is the foundational first step. Self-awareness emerges as a cornerstone of effective leadership within an organization. As self-aware leaders, we possess a profound understanding of our strengths and weaknesses, enabling us to leverage strengths and address weaknesses proactively. This self-awareness nurtures authenticity, allowing us to lead with genuineness and integrity, thus earning the trust and respect of our team members. Self-awareness also better equips us to navigate challenges and conflicts by recognizing our biases and emotional triggers. This awareness empowers us to approach situations with clarity and objectivity. Self-awareness also facilitates continuous growth and development by acknowledging areas for improvement and actively seeking feedback and learning opportunities.

Believing in ourselves and our abilities is essential for navigating life's uncertainties and challenges with confidence and resilience. Many women struggle with feelings of inadequacy or self-doubt, fearing they will be exposed as frauds despite their accomplishments. Our thoughts have a significant impact on our confidence level, as they carry energy that can either boost or diminish our self-assurance. This energy is often influenced by our beliefs, which shape the signals we send to others about our confidence. It's crucial to identify and address any limiting beliefs to shift the energy we project. Practicing self-compassion and recognizing our achievements can also help us overcome self-doubt and cultivate confidence. When we have self-belief, we develop inner assurance and conviction, empowering us to step outside our comfort zones and take calculated risks. This belief becomes a driving force, propelling us toward our goals and aspirations, even amid uncertainty or adversity. With self-belief, we're more likely to seize opportunities as pathways to growth and fulfillment, rather than sources of fear or doubt. In the face of obstacles or setbacks, a strong belief in ourselves provides the resilience needed to persevere and overcome challenges. Rather than succumbing to self-doubt, we draw upon our inner strength and determination to navigate difficulties, learn from experiences, and emerge stronger. Ultimately, believing in ourselves not only unlocks our potential but also fosters a mindset of empowerment that enables us to embrace the journey of self-discovery, growth, and achievement with courage and conviction.

Clarifying our purpose and aligning our actions with our values serves as a compass, guiding us toward meaningful achievements and a sense of fulfillment in both our personal and professional endeavors. When we take the time to reflect on our purpose—our reason for being—and identify the values that resonate deeply with us, we gain clarity about what truly matters to us. This clarity provides a clear sense of direction, helping us prioritize our goals and make decisions that are in alignment with our aspirations and principles. When our actions are congruent with our values, we experience a profound sense of authenticity and integrity, which fuels our motivation and commitment to pursue our objectives with passion and determination. Rather than being driven solely by external markers of success, such as wealth or status, aligning our actions with our values enables us to derive intrinsic satisfaction from our efforts, knowing that they are contributing to a greater purpose or cause that is meaningful to us. In this way, clarifying our purpose and living in accordance with our values not only provides a sense of direction and motivation but also fosters a deeper sense of fulfillment and purpose in our lives.

Adaptability is the cornerstone of success in today's fast-paced and ever-changing world, as it empowers us to navigate uncertainty with agility and resilience. By embracing change and remaining open to new ideas and experiences, we position ourselves to thrive in dynamic environments where constant evolution is the norm. Rather than resisting or fearing change, adaptable women view it as an opportunity for growth and innovation. We can then approach new situations with a sense of curiosity and optimism, recognizing that each challenge presents a chance to learn and adapt. This openness enables us to stay ahead of the curve, anticipate emerging trends, and seize opportunities that others may overlook. Adaptability also fosters versatility, enabling us to pivot quickly when circumstances shift and to leverage our skills and strengths in diverse contexts. In essence, by embracing change and remaining flexible, we not only navigate uncertainty with greater ease but also position ourselves to capitalize on emerging opportunities, driving our personal and professional growth in dynamic and transformative ways.

Developing empathy toward others is another foundation of effective leadership, as it lays the foundation for strong relationships, fosters effective communication, and drives collaborative problem-solving. When we cultivate empathy, we develop a deep understanding of the thoughts, feelings, and perspectives of those around us, allowing us to connect with them on a deeper level. This connection forms the basis of trust and mutual respect, essential ingredients for building strong relationships in the workplace and beyond. Empathy enhances communication by allowing us to tailor messages with clarity and compassion. By listening actively and showing empathy, we create inclusive environments where team members feel valued and understood, promoting openness and collaboration. Empathy also encourages considering diverse viewpoints in problem-solving, leading to innovative solutions. Ultimately, cultivating empathy strengthens leadership impact by fostering trust, collaboration, and empathy within teams and companies.

The ability to combine kindness with the courage to have truthful, difficult conversations is a powerful leadership trait that can inspire trust, respect, and growth among team members. Engaging in truthful, difficult conversations with our staff demonstrates kindness in a profound way. While it may seem uncomfortable or even challenging in the moment, addressing issues openly and honestly shows respect for the individual and the team as a whole. It's an act of genuine care and consideration for their growth and development. This approach showcases real confidence on the part of the leader. It takes courage and self-assurance to confront difficult topics directly, rather than avoiding them or sugar-coating the truth. By having these difficult conversations, we demonstrate our belief in our own ability to handle tough situations and our commitment to fostering a culture of transparency and accountability within the team.

Cultivating gratitude is transformative, enriching our lives and fueling our ability to achieve success. It shifts our focus from scarcity to abundance, fostering resilience and contentment. By celebrating our accomplishments, big and small, we build confidence and self-worth. Gratitude for experiences, positive and negative, fosters growth and wisdom. It strengthens relationships, deepening connections and enhancing well-being. Gratitude also nurtures a positive outlook, fueling our inner power and inspiring courage and creativity in facing challenges. Ultimately, cultivating gratitude empowers us to create meaningful successes in both our personal and professional lives.

Creating a clear vision for our future is essential. It not only illuminates our path but also inspires and motivates us to reach our potential. With a clear vision, we can set ambitious goals, providing a roadmap for progress and driving continuous improvement. A compelling vision also inspires others, fostering a shared sense of purpose and commitment. Mobilizing collective efforts toward shared objectives harnesses the power of collaboration, leading to collective success and fulfillment.

Practicing self-discipline is key to maintaining focus, productivity, and accountability in both personal and professional realms. It involves setting clear priorities and boundaries, allocating time and energy effectively, and resisting distractions. By establishing specific goals and deadlines, we create a framework for action, staying motivated to achieve desired outcomes. Managing resources with discipline ensures prudent decisions and maximizes efficiency. Ultimately, self-discipline cultivates habits of self-control, responsibility, and consistency, enhancing productivity, performance, and overall fulfillment.

In the face of constant change and uncertainty, embracing self-compassion offers a vital anchor, allowing us to navigate challenges with kindness and understanding toward ourselves. Rather than being consumed by self-criticism or fear of failure, self-compassion encourages us to acknowledge our humanity with gentleness and empathy, cultivating resilience and a growth mindset. Approaching ourselves and our experiences with compassion creates a supportive inner environment that fosters curiosity, experimentation, and creative thinking, enabling us to adapt to changing circumstances and seize opportunities with more confidence. Ultimately, embracing self-compassion fosters well-being, personal growth, resilience, and creativity needed to thrive in an ever-evolving world.

Embracing lifelong learning is vital in today's fast-paced world, where constant change and innovation are the norm. Committing to continuous personal development enables us to stay relevant, innovative, and adaptable amidst uncertainty and disruption. It cultivates curiosity, fosters openness to new ideas, and equips us to anticipate emerging trends and solve complex problems. This mindset not only enhances resilience and adaptability but also fuels creativity and innovation, empowering us to thrive in an ever-changing landscape. Ultimately, lifelong learning empowers us to navigate uncertainty with more confidence and seize opportunities for success and fulfillment in both our personal and professional lives.

Understanding the systemic biases and cultural barriers behind the gender gap in C-suite roles is pivotal for driving meaningful organizational change. Fueled by entrenched gender norms and stereotypes, these biases reinforce the perception of leadership as inherently masculine, leading to unconscious bias in recruitment, promotion, and retention processes. Persistent obstacles, like unequal mentorship, limited visibility in decision-making spheres, and the absence of supportive policies such as flexible work arrangements, hinder women's access to high-level opportunities. Cultural norms favoring long hours and in-office presence further disadvantage women, especially those juggling career advancement with caregiving responsibilities, also perpetuates gender inequality in upper leadership levels.

To counter these challenges, we can take proactive steps to cultivate real confidence and navigate our careers authentically, resiliently, and assertively in a collaborative rather than competitive manner. Building supportive networks through mentorship relationships, peer support, and professional associations provides invaluable guidance and camaraderie.

Prioritizing self-care through routines, boundaries, and work-life balance is essential for sustaining well-being amidst professional demands. For instance, establishing personal boundaries is an act of self-care and self-respect, as they delineate the level of respect and consideration we expect from others. Flexible and well-defined boundaries offer a sense of control, providing more certainty, consistency, and confidence. This enables us to detach ourselves from situations, facilitating conscious decision-making free from emotions. As leaders, having adaptable boundaries allows us to tailor our approach, respond constructively to criticism or objections, and navigate negotiations and discussions with flexibility. By maintaining flexibility in our boundaries, we foster a more personalized leadership style and effectively manage expectations.

Attending outcome-based empowerment workshops or conferences offers inspiration and practical strategies to start addressing challenges such as self-doubt, gender bias, limited mentorship opportunities, work-life balance issues, lack of visibility, decision-making hesitancy, perfectionism, etc., ultimately unlocking our full leadership potential and contributing to organizational success.

Collaboration between aspiring leaders and inclusive companies is vital for driving progress and fostering change. Partnering with inclusive companies grants women access to valuable resources, benefiting both parties through diverse perspectives and enhanced innovation. Together, we create a supportive environment where women can thrive through solidarity and shared expertise. As women, we must also take proactive ownership of our career by actively engaging in opportunities, seeking clarity on policies, etc.

Professional development initiatives tailored for women, such as leadership development programs or career advancement programs with a focus on cultivating real confidence, can significantly empower women to unleash their full potential within corporate environments. As we've explored the principles of real confidence, it's evident that investing in personal development and coaching services focused on cultivating this inner strength is essential for women aspiring to leadership roles. These services provide invaluable guidance, support, and tools to unlock their full potential and overcome common challenges. Early investment in professional and coaching services offers significant benefits for both individuals and companies. By providing support and resources upfront, women are better prepared and aligned to pursue leadership roles with confidence and clarity. This proactive investment not only saves companies money by ensuring the right fit for leadership positions but also reduces stress and frustration for women who may later realize that pursuing C-suite roles isn't aligned with their aspirations.

Collaboration between women and companies advances leadership progress, fostering resilience, empowerment, and continuous learning. The path to C-suite positions for women requires resilience, authenticity, continuous learning, and above all, a profound level of confidence that enables them to navigate complexities with courage and integrity.

We must continue to proactively pursue our career goals, advocating for ourselves and seizing growth opportunities. By embracing our authenticity and building real confidence, we can lead effectively, driving positive change and inspiring future leaders. We can also cultivate an inclusive, empowering corporate culture by championing supportive practices and investing in our development, breaking barriers and reshaping the landscape of leadership. It's time to embrace our power and pave the way for a more diverse, equitable, and inclusive future in business!

In conclusion, cultivating real confidence is essential for women navigating the corporate landscape or entrepreneurship. If you're ready to uncover your path with clarity and confidence, visit https://bit.ly/RisetoLead-BuildingLeadershipfromWithin.

I also invite Corporate and Human Resources Executives to connect with me at lynn@realbizconfidence.com to explore how I can assist your organization in empowering your female workforce. Proactively investing in personal leadership training and coaching will better ensure alignment and readiness for those poised to pursue leadership roles, benefiting both your staff and the organization.

Dr. Victoria Stakelum

The Success Smith
Success Mindset Expert

https://www.linkedin.com/in/victoriastakelum/
https://www.facebook.com/groups/successcollective
https://www.instagram.com/thesuccesssmith/
https://www.thesuccesssmith.com/
https://leadership.scoreapp.com/

Dr Victoria Stakelum is a multi-award winning psychologist, leadership expert and NLP Master Coach. She had a hugely successful leadership career, becoming an Executive Shareholder and Deputy Chief Executive before her 40th Birthday – alongside raising three children. Victoria has received accolades as an 'Inspirational Woman in Business' for her role in launching and leading Arden University – once a lossmaking £6m turnover online education business, now a £150m global online and blended Higher Education institution of renown. She attributes her success to her engagement with mindfulness and self-development practices - this enabled her to move through the pressures and challenges of top leadership in high growth, demanding environments with confidence, ease and composure – a capability she is passionate to see more women develop. She now runs her own business, helping women heal their self-worth and confidence wounds and develop the skillset and mindset to achieve fulfilment and success in both leadership and life.

KNOW THYSELF

By Dr. Victoria Stakelum

Top leadership is tough. There are no two ways about it.

You are responsible for tens, hundreds, maybe thousands of people's employment.

You carry significant pressure from shareholders.

You are in the public eye representing your organisation.

People look to you for guidance and direction.

You are expected to deliver performance and profit – and the consequences of failing to do so can be severe – financially, reputationally, and emotionally.

Whilst the benefits can be significant, the challenges are undeniable.

And as a woman, a whole additional layer of complexity exists.

Your appearance may be scrutinised and commented on.

You are expected to maintain a beautiful, clean home.

You are likely to be carrying the primary caring responsibilities for children, if you have them.

If you have a bad day and get upset or angry or if you show vulnerability or let the stress get to you, you are seen as an "over-emotional woman." But if you speak too firmly, show aggression, or make "hard-nosed decisions," you are branded a bitch.

Is it any wonder so few women make it to the top table and stay there?!

My name is Dr Victoria Stakelum:

I landed my first executive role as Group Strategic Marketing Director for a £100m turnover global business aged, 34.

At 37, I became an Executive Director and Shareholder.

At 39, I was appointed Deputy Chief Executive of the fastest growing Private University in the world.

Until the final 2 years of my corporate career, I was always the only woman on the board.

I had three children, sang in a band, and went to the gym.

I narrowly avoided burnout.

How?

How was I able to achieve such leadership success *without* sacrificing balance?

In this chapter, I want to share insights on the psychology and energy of achieving leadership success as a woman – and how to do that on your own terms.

The Problem with Power

I regularly run leadership seminars for women. I'll often start with an exercise to flush out limiting beliefs and unhelpful associations with leadership.

Let's try it together now…

What feelings come up for you when I ask…

How do you feel about having ***power*** over others?

How do you feel about carrying lots of ***responsibility?***

How do you feel about having *authority?*

For many women I speak to, these words bring up fear and negativity.

"I don't like the idea of power – it's not how I'd want to lead"

"I couldn't handle more responsibility – I'm already stressed!"

"I associate authority with people in my past who have not treated me well"

What came up for you?

Did you feel resistance bubble up?

Make no mistake: leadership involves power, responsibility, and authority.

Our subtle subconscious associations with power and authority can block us from reaching senior positions without us even being aware of them.

Many of us, deep down, believe that power and authority are inherently wrong or bad.

We develop these beliefs during childhood. We are told "Stop being bossy", "You're too argumentative", and "Can't you just sit still?"

The schooling system teaches us to sit quietly and work hard – if we are loud, opinionated, or strong-willed, we are seen as troublemakers – not future leaders. These narratives are reinforced during adulthood as we look at the sources of power and authority around us and very often dislike what we see. When you consider the behaviours of many political and business leaders today is it any wonder that we form such negative views of power? All around us, we see it being wielded with little integrity or care.

So we come to believe that leadership is not for girls, and that power is bad.

Contrast this with the concept of "empowerment." I have noticed through my work that women are often more comfortable with the concept of being *empowered* than of being *powerful.*

To me, this is an interesting distinction.

The Oxford Dictionary's definition of power is

"The capacity or ability to direct or influence the behaviour of others or the course of events"

Whereas empowerment is defined as

"Authority or power given to someone to do something"

So to be empowered is to be *given* power.

By rejecting *power* but accepting *empowerment,* we are awaiting permission to direct or influence people and events.

But when we believe in our own ability and right to exert influence, we no longer need to wait for permission from someone else.

I truly believe that women will thrive in leadership when we stop waiting for permission to step up to power and begin embracing it. It starts with realising that power itself is not a bad thing – it is what is done with power that matters.

Think of a knife. It can be used to cause great harm or it can be used to carve great beauty. It can even be used to spread delicious jam onto toast! The knife is not the problem – what matters is the intention of the person holding it.

When we see so much power wielded badly, we feel reluctant to step into positions that grant us that power or associate us with it in any way.

But it doesn't have to be this way! If we can embrace power, we can become the knife that carves beauty rather than causes harm.

So say it with me:

"It is ok for me to become powerful. Because my intention is good and I will hold my power with care and integrity."

My own experience of being "power-full" was a highly rewarding one. From my position of authority, I was able to make positive changes. I could improve cultures, build diverse leadership teams, and help the next generation of leaders succeed. By leading in a way that brought both confidence <u>and</u> integrity, I was able to create high-performance businesses in which people and profit went hand in hand.

This was only possible because I was willing to embrace power. I felt motivated to keep progressing up the career ladder because I saw how much good I could achieve from these powerful positions.

I encountered bad leaders on occasion and to me, it seemed clear that poor leadership and inappropriate uses of power always led to poor performance and people issues, which ultimately cost businesses money.

Leaders with little self-awareness, badly regulated emotions, fragile egos, insecurities, or who don't know how to get the best from others, couldn't help but create toxic environments and poor performance.

This is why a willingness to do the "inner work" is so vital to our becoming good leaders. Even when our intentions are good, low confidence, latent emotional baggage, or unhealed childhood wounds, can trigger behaviours that negatively affect a leader's credibility, composure, and ability to sustain personal and team performance.

So how do we release our negative associations with power and heal the wounds of our past?

How do we build our self-esteem and learn to wear our authority with ease and confidence?

And how do we handle the pressure of responsibility without stress and other overwhelming emotions tripping us up?

…So that more of us can reach and succeed in top leadership positions and create the kinds of positive, collaborative, and inclusive cultures that seem to come so naturally to female leaders?

Let's look at each of these themes in turn and explore the approaches you can take.

1. How to release your negative associations with power and heal the wounds of your past

A great starting point is to explore where your beliefs about power come from. Childhood experiences with authority figures such as parents and teachers can leave lasting wounds and create negative associations with power.

Think back to where you learned what power meant and how that might underpin the beliefs you have now.

How have you generalised those experiences to mean "all power is bad"?

Could you reframe "powerful people behave badly" to "that powerful person behaved badly – I get to do differently."

Think about your adult experiences and observations about people in power. What do you notice about the leaders you've experienced? How have they used their authority? How has this shaped your beliefs about leadership?

Similarly, bring awareness to those types of behaviour or interaction that bring up overwhelming emotions or reactions within you.

What do these remind you of?

Where are you reacting in ways that suggest a deeper wound is activated?

Can you begin noticing these moments and observing patterns in your own behaviour that highlight something that needs to be healed?

What do you need to let go of in order to move forward with more power, confidence, and resilience?

Finally, create your own definition of what brilliant, high-integrity leadership means to you. If you accept that leadership involves power, ask how you would love to use your power in positive ways.

What is the leadership legend you would love to create?

What legacy would you love to leave?

How could you hold yourself to this gold standard every single day of your career?

How will you positively engage the people around you in your vision, plans, and performance so that rather than being forced to perform or comply, they feel inspired and excited to be a part of your team or business?

2. How to build your self-esteem and wear your authority with ease and confidence

A key concept when it comes to breaking through the glass ceiling is that of I-shaped versus T-shaped leadership. I have supported hundreds of women approaching top leadership who have become stuck at the Head of Function level because they are locked into I-shaped leadership thinking.

Let me explain:

As we progress through our careers, most of us will reach I-shaped leadership at some point. The I-shape reflects our deep expertise in a particular subject matter specialism.

When I was a Marketing Director, I was an I-shaped leader. I was the most experienced when it came to marketing. My team would come to me for answers. I had expert subject matter knowledge and my most valued opinions came from my deep understanding of my field. Inevitably then, I attributed my value to my expertise. However, research shows that it is this overvaluing of expertise that often keeps women stuck[1].

Compare this with T-shaped leadership. A T-shaped leader has also come up through a specific function. But at some point along their leadership journey, they have broadened out to take on additional functions – usually fields in which they lack expertise.

Think about it. Every CEO you've ever worked for was I-shaped at one point. Perhaps they led Finance, Sales, or Operations and developed expertise in that one function. Even if they had some experience in another area, they would almost never have expertise in all of the functions they held responsibility for as the top leader.

For example, in my role as a Deputy Chief Executive, I was responsible for Marketing, Sales, HR, IT, Customer Experience, and Operations. I had deep expertise in marketing and customer experience and about a year of sales experience. But HR, IT, and Ops? These were completely new to me when I took them on.

For many women, this is a breakpoint moment. Line managing people "better" than us in their fields can bring up massive imposter syndrome. Our feeling of personal value can plummet when we are no longer the expert in the room. This can collapse our confidence, create feelings of pressure, and bring up insecurities we didn't know we had. It is particularly acute for high-achieving women who have never really allowed themselves to fail or be seen to struggle. Those childhood

---

[1] Helgesen, Sally, and Marshall Goldsmith. How women rise: Break the 12 habits holding you back. London: Random House Business Books, 2019.

wounds that left us feeling inadequate, unlovable, or not good enough can come back with a vengeance to leave us feeling lost, insecure, and overwhelmed.

For me, that moment came when I moved from Marketing Leadership into broader Commercial Leadership. Overnight, I was responsible for a sales function. I had almost zero experience in sales. And for the first time, I was managing people that had more expertise in their fields than I did.

Initially, I tried to solve all the problems. When targets weren't being met I cracked the whip harder, showed my frustration, and secretly worried that I was failing in my role.

After a couple of months of choppy waters I sat down with my team of functional managers and confessed that I felt completely lost. I asked them what they thought was going wrong and what ideas they had to turn the performance around. Together, we came up with new thinking. It unlocked the performance we needed.

This gave me a valuable lesson in both vulnerability and authenticity. I saw clearly that my role was no longer to have all the answers, but rather to ask the best questions and hold space for my more experienced colleagues to shape the solutions.

I was lucky that I had trained in coaching, had a well-developed mindfulness practice to help me steady my emotions when the going was getting tough, and I had a good rapport with my team.

This is key in T-shaped leadership – your job is not to have all the answers and drive all activities yourself. It is to create a clear vision, engage your people in that vision, and unlock *their* greatest potential in delivering that vision. The more you **tell**, the less room there is for you to unlock *their* expertise. The more curious and open you are, the more space you create for other people's brilliance to shine.

This can be hard! You have to be pretty secure in your own value to allow others to win the day. It is easy to feel threatened.

I had a client who was reluctant to delegate. This meant she was always run ragged – overworked, overwhelmed, barely able to think straight! Initially, it appeared that she didn't have people she could reliably delegate to. But over time, we uncovered that she was anxious about passing high-value projects to her team because they might outshine her. The unhealed part of her that feared being outshone was showing up for her and holding her back from reaching her own potential.

A profound shift for her came as she healed those long-held wounds, and learned that her own leadership value came not from her direct contribution, but from her skill in unlocking performance in her team. It was not about <u>what</u> she delivered, but rather <u>how</u> she showed up. As her team really began to thrive and deliver on her behalf, it freed up her time and energy to focus on more company-wide and strategic initiatives – which in turn further built her own visibility and value. She healed her insecurities and made the leap from I-shaped to T-shaped leadership – by learning to let go, think big, and switch her focus from delivery and projects to people and vision.

What do you need to let go of in order to become T-shaped?

3. How to handle the pressure of responsibility without stress and overwhelming emotions tripping us up?

Pressure is inevitable in high-profile, high-responsibility roles. But *stress* is optional. So how do you handle pressure without being stressed?

You've probably heard of the Oracle of Delphi. In ancient Greece, people visited the oracle to ask for guidance about their destiny or how to handle challenges. Above the entrance to the sacred oracle were inscribed two words:

"Know Thyself"

The best leaders – those who are composed, clear-headed, and create engaged high-performing teams – are those who know themselves deeply – their strengths and weaknesses, their traits and triggers.

To be a calm, successful leader, it is vital to look honestly at yourself and learn to accept and value yourself for both your talents *and* your weaknesses.

By forgiving yourself for mistakes and failures, you can focus on learning rather than losses.

By uncovering your emotional triggers, you can learn to see them coming and instead of reacting, choose a response – with clear intention and a focus on ideal outcomes.

In learning to accept yourself, you become kind of bulletproof.

No feedback can rock you if you have already looked at that weakness or mistake yourself.

No failure can shame you if you are no longer making it *mean something* about your value or worth.

No boundary can be blurred if you are no longer seeking external validation.

When you know and accept yourself completely you have nothing to prove.

Your motivation and energy now come from passion and commitment rather than from fear or frustration.

And this is the most important personal journey of leadership – that to self-acceptance.

This is not always an easy journey. We have blindspots, latent baggage, and emotional triggers that can affect our energy and performance. But walking the path is a hugely worthwhile journey and truly transformative – both professionally and personally.

A great starting point is to bracket each day with a reflection:

"How do I want to show up today?" Then "How did I do well today?" and "What did I get to learn?"

To go deeper, ask for feedback from a range of colleagues – ideally in a way that allows them to provide anonymous, honest feedback.

"How am I when I'm at my best?" "What would you love me to do more of?" and "What aspect of my leadership do you find least helpful?"

It takes courage to seek this feedback and having a coach support you through the process and findings can be helpful.

My mission is to support more leaders to heal and to develop the self-awareness, acceptance, and emotional mastery to lead with power, integrity, composure, **and** positive impact.

If you would value some support in exploring *your* blindspots and going on this journey, please don't hesitate to reach out for an informal discussion on how I may be able to help.

You can find me at https://thesuccesssmith.com

JOIN THE MOVEMENT!
#BAUW

Becoming An Unstoppable Woman
With She Rises Studios

She Rises Studios was founded by Hanna Olivas and Adriana Luna Carlos, the mother-daughter duo, in mid-2020 as they saw a need to help empower women worldwide. They are the podcast hosts of the *She Rises Studios Podcast* and Amazon best-selling authors and motivational speakers who travel the world. Hanna and Adriana are the movement creators of #BAUW - Becoming An Unstoppable Woman: The movement has been created to universally impact women of all ages, at whatever stage of life, to overcome insecurities, and adversities, and develop an unstoppable mindset. She Rises Studios educates, celebrates, and empowers women globally.

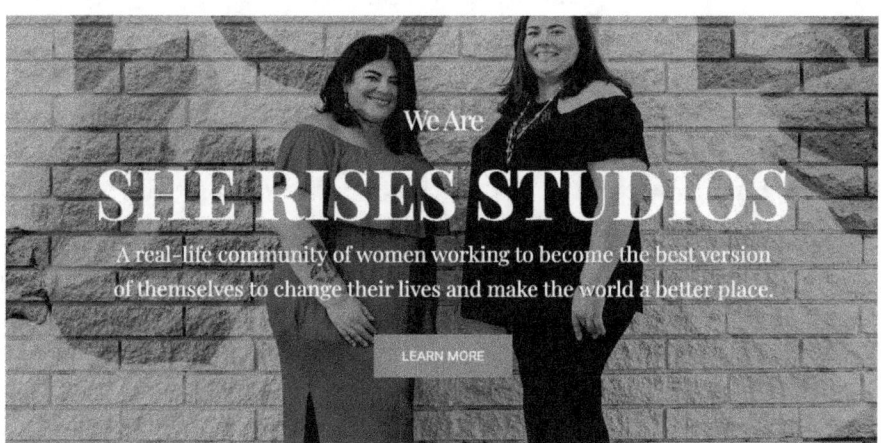

Looking to Join Us in our Next Anthology

or Publish YOUR Own?

She Rises Studios Publishing offers full-service publishing, marketing, book tour, and campaign services. For more information,

contact info@sherisesstudios.com

We are always looking for women who want to share their stories and expertise and feature their businesses on our podcasts, in our books, and in our magazines.

SEE WHAT WE DO

OUR PODCAST   **OUR BOOKS**   **OUR SERVICES**

Be featured in the Becoming An Unstoppable Woman magazine, published in 13 countries and sold in all major retailers. Get the visibility you need to LEVEL UP in your business!

Have your own TV show streamed across major platforms like

Roku TV, Amazon Fire Stick, Apple TV and more!

Learn to leverage your expertise. Build your online presence and grow your audience with FENIX TV.
https://fenixtv.sherisesstudios.com/

Visit www.SheRisesStudios.com to see how YOU can join the #BAUW movement and help your community to achieve the UNSTOPPABLE mindset.

Have you checked out the *She Rises Studios Podcast?*

Find us on all MAJOR platforms: Spotify, IHeartRadio, Apple Podcasts, Google Podcasts, etc.

Looking to become a sponsor or build a partnership?

Email us at info@sherisesstudios.com

SHE RISES
STUDIOS

www.ingramcontent.com/pod-product-compliance
Lightning Source LLC
Chambersburg PA
CBHW071023120626
46546CB00003B/1195